THE
DIARY OF
ANNE FRANK

STUDENT DRAMA SERIES

General Editor : MICHAEL MARLAND, B.A.

TITLES IN THE SERIES

THE
DIARY OF
ANNE FRANK

DRAMATIZED BY FRANCES GOODRICH
and
ALBERT HACKETT

BASED ON THE BOOK *Anne Frank: Diary of a Young Girl*

EDITED BY MICHAEL MARLAND, B.A.

With set designs by Bill Pinner
Photographs from a London production

BLACKIE *LONDON & GLASGOW*

Blackie & Son Limited
BISHOPBRIGGS, GLASGOW G64 2NZ
7 LEICESTER PLACE,
LONDON WC2H 7BP

THIS EDITION FIRST PUBLISHED 1970
0 216 87148 4

PRINTED IN GREAT BRITAIN BY
BELL AND BAIN LTD, GLASGOW

CONTENTS

ACKNOWLEDGMENTS

The editor is grateful to the following for their help in the preparation of this volume:

Frances Goodrich, Albert Hackett and Otto Frank for their permission to reprint *The Diary of Anne Frank*.
Dr. Otto Frank and Vallentine, Mitchell & Co. Limited for permission to reprint an extract from the book *The Diary of Anne Frank*.
Bill Pinner for the set designs.

The authors are grateful for the guidance of Dr. Otto H. Frank, Dr. L. de Jong, Miss Lidia Winkle and The Netherlands State Institute for War Documentation, Amsterdam, when working on the dramatization of the story.

INTRODUCTION

It's a long way from an ordinary German-Jewish family hiding from the Nazis in a Dutch attic in 1942 to reading or producing this play in English today. But the feeling of the young Anne and her growing understanding of life has lived through all those years—and through many versions. It was first recorded by Anne Frank herself in the diary she started on her thirteenth birthday. This was discovered after the war (as the first scene of the play shows) and published in Holland a few years later. By 1952, ten years after the first page had been written, it was translated into English and published in Britain; and four years after that two Americans adapted it into the play, which is published and is still often read and produced in many parts of the world.

The Frank family were Jews. They fled from Germany to Holland in 1933 to avoid the persecution of the Nazis, but in 1940 Holland was invaded and the persecution caught up with them again. The Jewish race was seen by the Nazi rulers as the enemies of Germany. The Jew was pictured on poster and propaganda sheet as the debaser of the 'purity' of the German race; every difficulty and evil was seen as the fault of the Jews and the whole government machine was behind the branding and attacking of the Jews. Even children's books were written that declared: 'The Jew is the devil in human form'. Hitler's last words before his death were to repeat the old message:

'I impose on the leadership and following of the nation the obligation to hold fast to the racial laws and to carry on unmerciful resistance to the world poisoner of all nations—international Jewry.'

The early policy of the Nazi party was to force emigration of Jews, but by 1941, the year before Anne started her diary, the decision has been taken to carry out the 'final solution' of the Jewish problem—extermination. The Jews were forced to wear a yellow star (the Star of David mentioned in the stage directions on page 4), and their lives were hounded by restrictions and unpleasantnesses. The threat of the 'final solution' was always closing in on them, and from time to time another group would be herded off to no one knew quite where—the gas chambers and mass shootings of the concentration camps.

Thousands of Jews went into hiding, and this play helps us to re-live the lives of eight, of whom Anne was the youngest, and her father was to be the only survivor. This is not a play where the 'excitement and tension' come from the fact that we don't know what is going to happen. The family did not survive, and the details of what happened after the beating on the door that closes the play are horrible: Van Daan was put to death in the gas chamber at Auschwitz; Anne's mother died after trying to stop an S.S. guard from assaulting her elder daughter, Margot; both Margot, first, and then Anne, died of typhus in the hell of Belsen. Anne died two months before the Netherlands were freed; she was aged fifteen years and nine months. All the others perished except the father, Otto Frank. He was in the hospital at Auschwitz when the Soviet armies reached the camp in January 1945; finally, with a few other survivors, he got to the Black Sea port of Odessa, where a New Zealand ship brought them back to Western Europe.

Anne started her diary while she was at school (the first pages are reprinted on page 102), and it is a double record. Firstly it tells of the effects of the German rule, a documentary of the methods and will to survive that were used in an attempt to escape death. For more than two years these eight human beings never went outdoors, kept completely silent for about ten hours a day when strangers were working in the warehouse downstairs, never stood by a window during daylight, never discarded rubbish that might betray them, never drew water or flushed the lavatory when there was anyone in the building.

But the diary was also a second kind of document, and this is also retained in the play: it was a sensitive record of the enthusiasm and growth of a young girl. She was clearly clever, and perhaps more grown-up in many ways than other girls of her age, and also she wanted to be a writer. But she was, despite the cramped and artificial cage, a normal girl exploring her feelings and thinking about her companions on the pages of her diary. In fact, the artificial cage had the effect of sharpening and focusing her reactions for the benefit of her diary.

The authors of this play wrote out of the diary, and out of

their knowledge of the attic and its neighbourhood, which they visited and studied. They met Anne's father (who was living in Switzerland), and his explanations and memories were woven into the play. They wrote eight drafts before it was ready for the stage, for a diary cannot be translated directly. For one thing, the diary was written by Anne, from *her* point of view. A play, on the other hand, must show Anne as one of the characters, and must allow us to view the other characters for ourselves— not through her eyes. Then the diary, like any other one, is fragmentary, goes back and forth, and has the shape only of the passing of time, whereas a play needs a satisfactory rhythm and shape for performance. Lastly, there was the difficult point that in a play descriptions and impressions have to be expressed by *incidents*: events and small happenings had to be invented to show the tensions and interplay of characters.

The Diary of Anne Frank allows the girl who was killed in 1945 to speak to us today of the harshness of war and the hopefulness of youth. The play reads effectively and can be staged movingly. After its performance in London, the dramatic critic J. C. Trewin, called this play 'One of the most astonishing documents of the war', and said: 'It is hard to write about the play because it is not so much a calculated piece for the stage as a document of an extraordinary experience'.

M.M.

PRONUNCIATION GUIDE

This is a list of all the German and Dutch names and words used in the play, with a rough guide to their pronunciation.

Amen	Oh-mein
Amsterdam	Ahm'-ster-dahm
Anne	Ah'-nah or the familiar Ah'-nee
Anneke	Ah'nah-kah
Anneline	Ah-nah-lynn
Auschwitz	Aow'-shvitz
Belsen	Bell'-sen
Buchenwald	Buch'-en-vald
Delphi	Dell'-fie
Dirk	Dee'-urk
Dussel	Duss'-ell
Edith	Ae'-dit
Frank	Frahnk
Hallensteins	Ha'-len-stains
Hilversum	Hill'-ver-sum
Jan	Yan
Jopie	Yo'-pee
Kerli	Care'-lee
Kraler	Krah'-ler
Liefje	Leaf'-yah
Margot	Mar'-gott
Mauthausen	Maut'-how-sen
Mazeltov	Mah'-zel-tahv
Miep	Meep
Mouschi	Moo'-shee
Otto	Ah'-toe
Peter	Pay'-ter
Petronella	Pet-row-nell'-ah
Putti	Poo'-tee
Rotterdam	Rah'-ter-dahm
Van Daan	Fahn Dahn
Wessels	Vess'-ells
Westertoren	Vess'-ter-tor-en
Wilhelmina	Vil-hel-mee'-nah

The Diary of Anne Frank

*by Frances Goodrich
and Albert Hackett*

For *GARSON KANIN*

The action takes place during the years of World War II, and immediately afterwards, in Amsterdam.

The play is divided into two Acts; although each of these has five scenes, there is no break within an Act. Each scene flows into the next, with the lights and sound cross-fading.

ACT 1

SCENE 1	November 1945	Late afternoon
SCENE 2	July 1942	Early morning
SCENE 3	August 1942	A few minutes after 6 p.m.
SCENE 4	September 1942	Midnight
SCENE 5	December 1942	Night

ACT 2

SCENE 1	January 1944	Late afternoon
SCENE 2	March 1944	Evening
SCENE 3	April 1944	Night
SCENE 4	July 1944	Afternoon
SCENE 5	November 1945	Late afternoon

THE CHARACTERS

MR. FRANK
MIEP
MRS. VAN DAAN
MR. VAN DAAN
PETER VAN DAAN
MRS. FRANK
MARGOT FRANK
ANNE FRANK
MR. KRALER
MR. DUSSEL

✳ ✳ ✳
Act 1

SCENE I

The scene remains the same throughout the play. It is the top floor of a warehouse and office building in Amsterdam, Holland. The sharply peaked roof of the building is outlined against a sea of other roof-tops, stretching away into the distance. Nearby is the belfry of a church tower, the Westertoren, whose carillon rings out the hours. Occasionally faint sounds float up from below: the voices of children playing in the street, the tramp of marching feet, a boat whistle from the canal.

The three rooms of the top floor and a small attic space above are exposed to our view. The largest of the rooms is in the centre, with two small rooms, slightly raised, on either side. On the right is a bathroom, out of sight. A narrow steep flight of stairs at the back leads up to the attic. The rooms are sparsely furnished with a few chairs, cots, a table or two. The windows are painted over, or covered with makeshift blackout curtains. In the main room there is a sink, a gas ring for cooking and a wood-burning stove for warmth.

The room on the left is hardly more than a cupboard. There is a skylight in the sloping ceiling. Directly under this room is a small steep stair-well, with steps leading down to a door. This is the only entrance from the building below. When the door is opened we see that it has been concealed on the outer side by a bookcase attached to it.

The curtain rises on an empty stage. It is late afternoon November, 1945.

The rooms are dusty, the curtains in rags. Chairs and tables are overturned.

The door at the foot of the small stair-well swings open. MR. FRANK *comes up the steps into view. He is a gentle, cultured European in his middle years. There is still a trace of a German accent in his speech.*

He stands looking slowly around, making a supreme effort at self-control. He is weak, ill. His clothes are threadbare.

After a second he drops his rucksack on the couch and moves slowly about. He opens the door to one of the smaller rooms, and then abruptly closes it again, turning away. He goes to the window at the back, looking off at the Westertoren as its carillon strikes the hour of six, then he moves restlessly on.

From the street below we hear the sound of a barrel organ and children's voices at play. There is a many-coloured scarf hanging from a nail. MR. FRANK *takes it, putting it around his neck. As he starts for his rucksack, his eye is caught by*

I

*something lying on the floor. It is a woman's white glove. He holds it in his hand
and suddenly all of his self-control is gone. He breaks down, crying.
We hear footsteps on the stairs. MIEP GIES comes up, looking for MR. FRANK.
MIEP is a Dutch girl of about twenty-two. She wears a coat and hat, ready to go
home. She is pregnant. Her attitude toward MR. FRANK is protective, compassionate.*

1 MIEP. Are you all right, Mr. Frank?

2 MR. FRANK [*quickly controlling himself*]. Yes, Miep, yes.

3 MIEP. Everyone in the office has gone home ... It's after six.
   [*then pleading*] Don't stay up here, Mr. Frank. What's the
   use of torturing yourself like this?

4 MR. FRANK. I've come to say good-bye ... I'm leaving here,
   Miep.

5 MIEP. What do you mean? Where are you going? Where?

6 MR. FRANK. I don't know yet. I haven't decided.

7 MIEP. Mr. Frank, you can't leave here! This is your home!
   Amsterdam is your home. Your business is here, waiting
   for you ... You're needed here ... Now that the war is
   over, there are things that ...

8 MR. FRANK. I can't stay in Amsterdam, Miep. It has too
   many memories for me. Everywhere there's something
   ... the house we lived in ... the school ... that street
   organ playing out there ... I'm not the person you
   used to know, Miep. I'm a bitter old man. [*breaking off*]
   Forgive me. I shouldn't speak to you like this ... after
   all that you did for us ... the suffering ...

9 MIEP. No. No. It wasn't suffering. You can't say we suffered.

   As she speaks, she straightens a chair which is overturned.

10 MR. FRANK. I know what you went through, you and Mr.
   Kraler. I'll remember it as long as I live. [*He gives one last
   look around.*] Come, Miep.

   *He starts for the steps, then remembers his rucksack, going back to get
   it.*

1   MIEP [*hurrying up to a cupboard*]. Mr. Frank, did you see? There
are some of your papers here. [*She brings a bundle of papers
to him.*] We found them in a heap of rubbish on the floor
after . . . after you left.

2   MR. FRANK. Burn them.

He opens his rucksack to put the glove in it.

3   MIEP. But, Mr. Frank, there are letters, notes . . .

4   MR. FRANK. Burn them. All of them.

5   MIEP. Burn *this*?

She hands him a paperbound notebook.

6   MR. FRANK [*quietly*]. Anne's diary. [*He opens the diary and begins
to read.*] 'Monday, the sixth of July, nineteen forty-two.'
[*to* MIEP] Nineteen forty-two. Is it possible, Miep? . . .
Only three years ago. [*As he continues his reading, he sits down
on the couch.*] 'Dear Diary, since you and I are going to be
great friends, I will start by telling you about myself. My
name is Anne Frank. I am thirteen years old. I was born
in Germany the twelfth of June, nineteen twenty-nine.
As my family is Jewish, we emigrated to Holland when
Hitler came to power.'

As MR. FRANK *reads on, another voice joins his, as if coming from
the air. It is* ANNE'S VOICE.

7   MR. FRANK AND ANNE. 'My father started a business, importing
spice and herbs. Things went well for us until nineteen
forty. Then the war came, and the Dutch capitulation,
followed by the arrival of the Germans. Then things got
very bad for the Jews.'

MR. FRANK'S VOICE *dies out.* ANNE'S VOICE *continues alone. The
lights dim slowly to darkness. The curtain falls on the scene.*

8   ANNE'S VOICE. You could not do this and you could not do
that. They forced Father out of his business. We had to
wear yellow stars. I had to turn in my bike. I couldn't
go to a Dutch school any more. I couldn't go to the

3

cinema, or ride in a motor car, or even on a streetcar, and a million other things. But somehow we children still managed to have fun. Yesterday Father told me we were going into hiding. Where, he wouldn't say. At five o'clock this morning Mother woke me and told me-to hurry and get dressed. I was to put on as many clothes as I could. It would look too suspicious if we walked along carrying suitcases. It wasn't until we were on our way that I learned where we were going. Our hiding place was to be upstairs in the building where Father used to have his business. Three other people were coming in with us . . . the Van Daans and their son Peter . . . Father knew the Van Daans but we had never met them . . .

During the last lines the curtain rises on the scene. The lights dim on. ANNE'S VOICE *fades out.*

SCENE 2

It is early morning, July, 1942. *The rooms are bare, as before, but they are now clean and orderly.*

MR. VAN DAAN, *a tall, portly man in his late forties, is in the main room, pacing up and down, nervously smoking a cigarette. His clothes and overcoat are expensive and well cut.*

MRS. VAN DAAN *sits on the couch, clutching her possessions, a hatbox, bags, etc. She is a pretty woman in her early forties. She wears a fur coat over her other clothes.*

PETER VAN DAAN *is standing at the window of the room on the right, looking down at the street below. He is a shy, awkward boy of sixteen. He wears a cap, a raincoat, and long Dutch trousers, like 'plus fours'. At his feet is a black case, a carrier for his cat.*

The yellow Star of David is conspicuous on all of their clothes.

2 MRS. VAN DAAN [*rising, nervous, excited*]. Something's happened to them! I know it!

3 MR. VAN DAAN. Now, Kerli!

4

1   MRS. VAN DAAN. Mr. Frank said they'd be here at seven
    o'clock. He said . . .

2   MR. VAN DAAN. They have two miles to walk. You can't
    expect . . .

3   MRS. VAN DAAN. They've been picked up. That's what's hap-
    pened. They've been taken . . .

    MR. VAN DAAN *indicates that he hears someone coming.*

4   MR. VAN DAAN. You see?

    PETER *takes up his carrier and his schoolbag, etc., and goes into the
    main room as* MR. FRANK *comes up the stair-well from below.* MR.
    FRANK *looks much younger now. His movements are brisk, his
    manner confident. He wears an overcoat and carries his hat and a
    small cardboard box. He crosses to the* VAN DAANS, *shaking hands
    with each of them.*

5   MR. FRANK. Mrs. Van Daan, Mr. Van Daan, Peter. [*then, in
    explanation of their lateness*] There were too many of the
    Green Police on the streets . . . we had to take the long
    way around.

    Up the steps come MARGOT FRANK, MRS. FRANK, MIEP (*not
    pregnant now*) and MR. KRALER. *All of them carry bags, packages,
    and so forth. The Star of David is conspicuous on all of the* FRANKS'
    clothing. MARGOT *is eighteen, beautiful, quiet, shy.* MRS. FRANK
    is a young mother, gently bred, reserved. She, like MR. FRANK,
    has a slight German accent. MR. KRALER *is a Dutchman, dependable,
    kindly.*
    As MR. KRALER *and* MIEP *go upstage to put down their parcels,*
    MRS. FRANK *turns back to call* ANNE.

6   MRS. FRANK. Anne?

    ANNE *comes running up the stairs. She is thirteen, quick in her
    movements, interested in everything, mercurial in her emotions. She
    wears a cape, long wool socks and carries a schoolbag.*

7   MR. FRANK [*introducing them*]. My wife, Edith. Mr. and Mrs.
    Van Daan [MRS. FRANK *hurries over, shaking hands with them*] . . .
    their son, Peter . . . my daughters, Margot and Anne.

ANNE gives a polite little curtsy as she shakes MR. VAN DAAN'S hand. Then she immediately starts off on a tour of investigation of her new home, going upstairs to the attic room.
MIEP and MR. KRALER are putting the various things they have brought on the shelves.

1 MR. KRALER. I'm sorry there is still so much confusion.

2 MR. FRANK. Please. Don't think of it. After all, we'll have plenty of leisure to arrange everything ourselves.

3 MIEP [*to MRS. FRANK*]. We put the stores of food you sent in here. Your drugs are here . . . soap, linen here.

4 MRS. FRANK. Thank you, Miep.

5 MIEP. I made up the beds . . . the way Mr. Frank and Mr. Kraler said. [*She starts out.*] Forgive me. I have to hurry. I've got to go to the other side of town to get some ration books for you.

6 MRS. VAN DAAN. Ration books? If they see our names on ration books, they'll know we're here.

7 MR. KRALER. There isn't anything . . .

8 MIEP. Don't worry. Your names won't be on them. [*As she hurries out.*] I'll be up later.   *together*

9 MR. FRANK. Thank you, Miep.

10 MRS. FRANK [*to MR. KRALER*]. It's illegal, then, the ration books? We've never done anything illegal.

11 MR. FRANK. We won't be living here exactly according to regulations.

As MR. KRALER reassures MRS. FRANK, he takes various small things, such as matches, soap, etc., from his pockets, handing them to her.

12 MR. KRALER. This isn't the black market, Mrs. Frank. This is what we call the white market . . . helping all of the hundreds and hundreds who are hiding out in Amsterdam.

The carillon is heard playing the quarter-hour before eight. MR.
KRALER *looks at his watch.* ANNE *stops at the window as she comes
down the stairs.*

1 ANNE. It's the Westertoren!

2 MR. KRALER. I must go. I must be out of here and downstairs
in the office before the workmen get here. [*He starts for
the stairs leading out.*] Miep or I, or both of us, will be up
each day to bring you food and news and find out what
your needs are. Tomorrow I'll get you a better bolt for
the door at the foot of the stairs. It needs a bolt that
you can throw yourself and open only at our signal.
[*to* MR. FRANK] Oh . . . You'll tell them about the noise?

3 MR. FRANK. I'll tell them.

4 MR. KRALER. Good-bye then for the moment. I'll come up
again, after the workmen leave.

5 MR. FRANK. Good-bye, Mr. Kraler.

6 MRS. FRANK [*shaking his hand*]. How can we thank you?

The others murmur their good-byes.

7 MR. KRALER. I never thought I'd live to see the day when a
man like Mr. Frank would have to go into hiding. When
you think—

He breaks off, going out. MR. FRANK *follows him down the steps,
bolting the door after him. In the interval before he returns,* PETER
goes over to MARGOT, *shaking hands with her. As* MR. FRANK *comes
back up the steps,* MRS. FRANK *questions him anxiously.*

8 MRS. FRANK. What did he mean, about the noise?

9 MR. FRANK. First let us take off some of these clothes.

*They all start to take off garment after garment. On each of their coats,
sweaters, blouses, suits, dresses, is another yellow Star of David.*
MR. *and* MRS. FRANK *are undressed quite simply. The others wear
several things, sweaters, extra dresses, bathrobes, aprons, nightgowns,
etc.*

7

1 MR. VAN DAAN. It's a wonder we weren't arrested, walking along the streets ... Petronella with a fur coat in July ... and that cat of Peter's crying all the way.

2 ANNE [*as she is removing a pair of panties*]. A cat?

3 MRS. FRANK [*shocked*]. Anne, please!

4 ANNE. It's all right. I've got on three more.

She pulls off two more. Finally, as they have all removed their surplus clothes, they look to MR. FRANK, *waiting for him to speak.*

5 MR. FRANK. Now. About the noise. While the men are in the building below, we must have complete quiet. Every sound can be heard down there, not only in the work-rooms, but in the offices too. The men come at about eight-thirty, and leave at about five-thirty. So, to be perfectly safe, from eight in the morning until six in the evening we must move only when it is necessary, and then in stocking-feet. We must not speak above a whisper. We must not run any water. We cannot use the sink, or even, forgive me, the W.C. The pipes go down through the workrooms. It would be heard. No rubbish ... [MR. FRANK *stops abruptly as he hears the sound of marching feet from the street below. Everyone is motionless, paralysed with fear.* MR. FRANK *goes quietly into the room on the right to look down out of the window.* ANNE *runs after him, peering out with him. The tramping feet pass without stopping. The tension is relieved.* MR. FRANK, *followed by* ANNE, *returns to the main room and resumes his instructions to the group.*] ... No rubbish, must ever be thrown out which might reveal that someone is living up here ... not even a potato peeling. We must burn everything in the stove at night. This is the way we must live until it is over, if we are to survive.

There is silence for a second.

6 MRS. FRANK. Until it is over.

7 MR. FRANK [*reassuringly*]. After six we can move about ... we can talk and laugh and have our supper and read and play games ... just as we would at home. [*He looks at his*

8

watch.] And now I think it would be wise if we all went to our rooms, and were settled before eight o'clock. Mrs. Van Daan, you and your husband will be upstairs. I regret that there's no place up there for Peter. But he will be here, near us. This will be our common room, where we'll meet to talk and eat and read, like one family.

2 MR. VAN DAAN. And where do you and Mrs. Frank sleep?

3 MR. FRANK This room is also our bedroom.

4 MRS. VAN DAAN. That isn't right. We'll sleep here and you take the room upstairs. ⎫
⎬ *together*
5 MR. VAN DAAN. It's your place. ⎭

6 MR. FRANK. Please. I've thought this out for weeks. It's the best arrangement. The only arrangement.

7 MRS. VAN DAAN [*to* MR. FRANK]. Never, never can we thank you. [*Then to* MRS. FRANK.] I don't know what would have happened to us, if it hadn't been for Mr. Frank.

8 MR. FRANK. You don't know how your husband helped me when I came to this country . . . knowing no one . . . not able to speak the language. I can never repay him for that. [*Going to* VAN DAAN.] May I help you with your things?

9 MR. VAN DAAN. No. No. [*to* MRS. VAN DAAN] Come along, *liefje.*

10 MRS. VAN DAAN. You'll be all right, Peter? You're not afraid?

11 PETER [*embarrassed*]. Please, Mother.

They start up the stairs to the attic room above. MR. FRANK *turns to* MRS. FRANK.

12 MR. FRANK. You too must have some rest, Edith. You didn't close your eyes last night. Nor you, Margot.

13 ANNE. I slept, Father. Wasn't that funny? I knew it was the last night in my own bed, and yet I slept soundly.

1 MR. FRANK. I'm glad, Anne. Now you'll be able to help me straighten things in here. [*to* MRS. FRANK *and* MARGOT] Come with me ... You and Margot rest in this room for the time being.

He picks up their clothes, starting for the room on the right.

2 MRS. FRANK. You're sure ... ? I could help ... And Anne hasn't had her milk ...

3 MR. FRANK. I'll give it to her. [*to* ANNE *and* PETER] Anne, Peter ... it's best that you take off your shoes now, before you forget.

He leads the way to the room, followed by MARGOT.

4 MRS. FRANK. You're sure you're not tired, Anne?

5 ANNE. I feel fine. I'm going to help Father.

6 MRS. FRANK. Peter, I'm glad you are to be with us.

7 PETER. Yes, Mrs. Frank.

MRS. FRANK *goes to join* MR. FRANK *and* MARGOT.
During the following scene MR. FRANK *helps* MARGOT *and* MRS. FRANK *to hang up their clothes. Then he persuades them both to lie down and rest. The* VAN DAANS *in their room above settle themselves. In the main room* ANNE *and* PETER *remove their shoes.* PETER *takes his cat out of the carrier.*

8 ANNE. What's your cat's name?

9 PETER. Mouschi.

10 ANNE. Mouschi! Mouschi! Mouschi! [*She picks up the cat, walking away with it. To* PETER] I love cats. I have one ... a darling little cat. But they made me leave her behind. I left some food and a note for the neighbours to take care of her ... I'm going to miss her terribly. What is yours? A him or a her?

11 PETER. He's a tom. He doesn't like strangers.

He takes the cat from her, putting it back in its carrier.

1 ANNE [*unabashed*]. Then I'll have to stop being a stranger, won't I? Is he fixed?

2 PETER [*startled*]. Huh?

3 ANNE. Did you have him fixed?

4 PETER. No.

5 ANNE. Oh, you ought to have him fixed—to keep him from —you know, fighting. Where did you go to school?

6 PETER. Jewish Secondary.

7 ANNE. But that's where Margot and I go! I never saw you around.

8 PETER. I used to see you . . . sometimes . . .

9 ANNE. You did?

10 PETER. . . . in the school yard. You were always in the middle of a bunch of kids.

He takes a penknife from his pocket.

11 ANNE. Why didn't you ever come over?

12 PETER. I'm sort of a lone wolf.

He starts to rip off his Star of David.

13 ANNE. What are you doing?

14 PETER. Taking it off.

15 ANNE. But you can't do that. They'll arrest you if you go out without your star.

He tosses his knife on the table.

16 PETER. Who's going out?

17 ANNE. Why, of course! You're right! Of course we don't need them any more. [*She picks up his knife and starts to take her star off.*] I wonder what our friends will think when we don't show up today?

11

1   PETER. I didn't have any dates with anyone.

2   ANNE. Oh, I did. I had a date with Jopie to go and play ping-pong at her house. Do you know Jopie de Waal?

3   PETER. No.

4   ANNE. Jopie's my best friend. I wonder what she'll think when she telephones and there's no answer? . . . Probably she'll go over to the house . . . I wonder what she'll think . . . we left everything as if we'd suddenly been called away . . . breakfast dishes in the sink . . . beds not made . . . [*As she pulls off her star the cloth underneath shows clearly the colour and form of the star.*] Look! It's still there! [PETER *goes over to the stove with his star.*] What're you going to do with yours?

5   PETER. Burn it.

6   ANNE [*She starts to throw hers in, and cannot*]. It's funny, I can't throw mine away. I don't know why.

7   PETER. You can't throw . . . ? Something they branded you with . . . ? That they made you wear so they could spit on you?

8   ANNE. I know. I know. But after all, it *is* the Star of David, isn't it?

    In the bedroom, right, MARGOT *and* MRS. FRANK *are lying down.* MR. FRANK *starts quietly out.*

9   PETER. Maybe it's different for a girl.

    MR. FRANK *comes into the main room.*

10 MR. FRANK. Forgive me, Peter. Now let me see. We must find a bed for your cat. [*He goes to a cupboard.*] I'm glad you brought your cat. Anne was feeling so badly about hers. [*getting a small worn wash-tub*] Here we are. Will it be comfortable in that?

11 PETER [*gathering up his things*]. Thanks.

1 MR. FRANK [*opening the door of the room on the left*]. And here is your room. But I warn you, Peter, you can't grow any more. Not an inch, or you'll have to sleep with your feet out of the skylight. Are you hungry?

2 PETER. No.

3 MR. FRANK. We have some bread and butter.

4 PETER. No, thank you.

5 MR. FRANK. You can have it for luncheon then. And tonight we will have a real supper . . . our first supper together.

6 PETER. Thanks. Thanks.

He goes into his room. During the following scene he arranges his possessions in his new room.

7 MR. FRANK. That's a nice boy, Peter.

8 ANNE. He's awfully shy, isn't he?

9 MR. FRANK. You'll like him, I know.

10 ANNE. I certainly hope so, since he's the only boy I'm likely to see for months and months.

MR. FRANK *sits down, taking off his shoes.*

11 MR. FRANK. Annele, there's a box there. Will you open it?

He indicates a carton on the couch. ANNE *brings it to the centre table. In the street below there is the sound of children playing.*

12 ANNE [*as she opens the carton*]. You know the way I'm going to think of it here? I'm going to think of it as a boarding house. A very peculiar summer boarding house, like the one that we—[*She breaks off as she pulls out some photographs.*] Father! My film stars! I was wondering where they were! I was looking for them this morning . . . and Queen Wilhelmina! How wonderful!

13 MR. FRANK. There's something more. Go on. Look further.

He goes over to the sink, pouring a glass of milk from a thermos bottle.

1   ANNE [*pulling out a pasteboard-bound book*]. A diary! [*She throws her arms around her father.*] I've never had a diary. And I've always longed for one. [*She looks around the room.*] Pencil, pencil, pencil, pencil. [*She starts down the stairs.*] I'm going down to the office to get a pencil.

2   MR. FRANK. Anne! No!

    He goes after her, catching her by the arm and pulling her back.

3   ANNE [*startled*]. But there's no one in the building now.

4   MR. FRANK. It doesn't matter. I don't want you ever to go beyond that door.

5   ANNE [*sobered*]. Never . . . ? Not even at night-time, when everyone is gone? Or on Sundays? Can't I go down to listen to the radio?

6   MR. FRANK. Never. I am sorry, Anneke. It isn't safe. No, you must never go beyond that door.

    For the first time ANNE *realizes what 'going into hiding' means.*

7   ANNE. I see.

8   MR. FRANK. It'll be hard, I know. But always remember this, Anneke. There are no walls, there are no bolts, no locks that anyone can put on your mind. Miep will bring us books. We will read history, poetry, mythology. [*He gives her the glass of milk.*] Here's your milk. [*With his arm about her, they go over to the couch, sitting down side by side.*] As a matter of fact, between us, Anne, being here has certain advantages for you. For instance, you remember the battle you had with your mother the other day on the subject of overshoes? You said you'd rather die than wear overshoes? But in the end you had to wear them? Well now, you see, for as long as we are here you will never have to wear overshoes! Isn't that good? And the coat that you inherited from Margot, you won't have to wear that any more. And the piano! You won't have to practise on the piano. I tell you, this is going to be a fine life for you!

14

ANNE'S panic is gone. PETER *appears in the doorway of his room, with a saucer in his hand. He is carrying his cat.*

1   PETER. I . . . I . . . I thought I'd better get some water for Mouschi before . . .

2   MR. FRANK. Of course.

As he starts towards the sink the carillon begins to chime the hour of eight. He tiptoes to the window at the back and looks down at the street below. He turns to PETER, *indicating in pantomime that it is too late.* PETER *starts back for his room. He steps on a creaking board. The three of them are frozen for a minute in fear. As* PETER *starts away again,* ANNE *tiptoes over to him and pours some of the milk from her glass into the saucer for the cat.* PETER *squats on the floor, putting the milk before the cat.* MR. FRANK *gives* ANNE *his fountain pen, and then goes into the room at the right. For a second* ANNE *watches the cat, then she goes over to the centre table, and opens her diary.*

In the room at the right, MRS. FRANK *has sat up quickly at the sound of the carillon.* MR. FRANK *comes in and sits down beside her on the couch, his arm comfortingly around her.*

Upstairs, in the attic room, MR. *and* MRS. VAN DAAN *have hung their clothes in the cupboard and are now seated on the iron bed.* MRS. VAN DAAN *leans back exhausted.* MR. VAN DAAN *fans her with a newspaper.*

ANNE *starts to write in her diary. The lights dim out, the curtain falls. In the darkness* ANNE'S VOICE *comes to us again, faintly at first, and then with growing strength.*

3   ANNE'S VOICE. I expect I should be describing what it feels like to go into hiding. But I really don't know yet myself. I only know it's funny never to be able to go outdoors . . . never to breathe fresh air . . . never to run and shout and jump. It's the silence in the nights that frightens me most. Every time I hear a creak in the house, or a step on the street outside, I'm sure they're coming for us. The days aren't so bad. At least we know that Miep and Mr. Kraler are down there below us in the office. Our protectors, we call them. I asked Father what would happen to them if the Nazis found out they were hiding us. Pim said that they would suffer the same fate

that we would . . . Imagine! They know this, and yet when they come up here, they're always cheerful and gay as if there were nothing in the world to bother them . . . Friday, the twenty-first of August, nineteen forty-two. Today I'm going to tell you our general news. Mother is unbearable. She insists on treating me like a baby, which I loathe. Otherwise things are going better. The weather is . . .

As ANNE'S VOICE *is fading out, the curtain rises on the scene.*

SCENE 3

It is a little after six o'clock in the evening, two months later.
MARGOT *is in the bedroom at the right, studying.* MR. VAN DAAN *is lying down in the attic room above.*
The rest of the 'family' is in the main room. ANNE *and* PETER *sit opposite each other at the centre table, where they have been doing their lessons.* MRS. FRANK *is on the couch.* MRS. VAN DANN *is seated with her fur coat, on which she has been sewing, in her lap. None of them are wearing their shoes.*
Their eyes are on MR. FRANK, *waiting for him to give them the signal which will release them from their day-long quiet.* MR. FRANK, *his shoes in his hand, stands looking down out of the window at the back, watching to be sure that all of the workmen have left the building below.*
After a few seconds of motionless silence, MR. FRANK *turns from the window.*

2 MR. FRANK [*quietly, to the group*]. It's safe now. The last workman has left.

There is an immediate stir of relief.

3 ANNE [*her pent-up energy exploding*]. WHEE!

4 MRS. FRANK [*startled, amused*]. Anne!

5 MRS. VAN DAAN. I'm first for the W.C.

She hurries off to the bathroom. MRS. FRANK *puts on her shoes and starts up to the sink to prepare supper.* ANNE *sneaks* PETER'S *shoes*

from under the table and hides them behind her back. MR. FRANK
goes into MARGOT'S *room.*

1 MR. FRANK [*to* MARGOT]. Six o'clock. School's over.

   MARGOT *gets up, stretching.* MR. FRANK *sits down to put on his
shoes. In the main room* PETER *tries to find his.*

2 PETER [*to* ANNE]. Have you seen my shoes?

3 ANNE [*innocently*]. Your shoes?

4 PETER. You've taken them, haven't you?

5 ANNE. I don't know what you're talking about.

6 PETER. You're going to be sorry!

7 ANNE. Am I?

   PETER *goes after her.* ANNE, *with his shoes in her hand, runs from
him, dodging behind her mother.*

8 MRS. FRANK [*protesting*]. Anne, dear!

9 PETER. Wait till I get you!

10 ANNE. I'm waiting! [PETER *makes a lunge for her. They both fall to
the floor.* PETER *pins her down, wrestling with her to get the shoes.*]
Don't! Don't! Peter, stop it. Ouch!

11 MRS. FRANK. Anne! . . . Peter!

   Suddenly PETER *becomes self-conscious. He grabs his shoes roughly
and starts for his room.*

12 ANNE [*following him*]. Peter, where are you going? Come dance
with me.

13 PETER. I tell you I don't know how.

14 ANNE. I'll teach you.

15 PETER. I'm going to give Mouschi his dinner.

16 ANNE. Can I watch?

C

1 PETER. He doesn't like people around while he eats.

2 ANNE. Peter, please.

3 PETER. No!

He goes into his room. ANNE *slams his door after him.*

4 MRS. FRANK. Anne, dear, I think you shouldn't play like that with Peter. It's not dignified.

5 ANNE. Who cares if it's dignified? I don't want to be dignified.

MR. FRANK *and* MARGOT *come from the room on the right.* MARGOT *goes to help her mother.* MR. FRANK *starts for the centre table to correct* MARGOT'S *school papers.*

6 MRS. FRANK [*to* ANNE]. You complain that I don't treat you like a grown-up. But when I do, you resent it.

7 ANNE. I only want some fun ... someone to laugh and clown with . . . After you've sat still all day and hardly moved, you've got to have some fun. I don't know what's the matter with that boy.

8 MR. FRANK. He isn't used to girls. Give him a little time.

9 ANNE. Time? Isn't two months time? I could cry. [*catching hold of* MARGOT] Come on, Margot . . . dance with me. Come on, please.

10 MARGOT. I have to help with supper.

11 ANNE. You know we're going to forget how to dance . . . When we get out we won't remember a thing.

She starts to sing and dance by herself. MR. FRANK *takes her in his arms, waltzing with her.* MRS. VAN DAAN *comes in from the bedroom.*

12 MRS. VAN DAAN. Next? [*She looks around as she starts putting on her shoes.*] Where's Peter?

13 ANNE [*as they are dancing*]. Where would he be!

18

1 MRS. VAN DAAN. He hasn't finished his lessons, has he? His father'll kill him if he catches him in there with that cat and his work not done. [MR. FRANK *and* ANNE *finish their dance. They bow to each other with extravagant formality.*] Anne, get him out of there, will you?

2 ANNE [*at* PETER's *door*]. Peter? Peter?

3 PETER [*opening the door a crack*]. What is it?

4 ANNE. Your mother says to come out.

5 PETER. I'm giving Mouschi his dinner.

6 MRS. VAN DAAN. You know what your father says.

She sits on the couch, sewing on the lining of her fur coat.

7 PETER. For heaven's sake, I haven't even looked at him since lunch.

8 MRS. VAN DAAN. I'm just telling you, that's all.

9 ANNE. I'll feed him.

10 PETER. I don't want you in there.

11 MRS. VAN DAAN. Peter!

12 PETER [*to* ANNE]. Then give him his dinner and come right out, you hear?

He comes back to the table. ANNE *shuts the door of* PETER's *room after her and disappears behind the curtain covering his closet.*

13 MRS. VAN DAAN [*to* PETER]. Now is that any way to talk to your little girl friend?

14 PETER. Mother ... for heaven's sake ... will you please stop saying that?

15 MRS. VAN DAAN. Look at him blush! Look at him!

16 PETER. Please! I'm not ... anyway ... let me alone, will you?

17 MRS. VAN DAAN. He acts like it was something to be ashamed of. It's nothing to be ashamed of, to have a little girl friend.

1 PETER. You're crazy. She's only thirteen.

2 MRS. VAN DAAN. So what? And you're sixteen. Just perfect.
Your father's ten years older than I am. [to MR. FRANK]
I warn you, Mr. Frank, if this war lasts much longer,
we're going to be related and then . . .

3 MR. FRANK. *Mazeltov!*

4 MRS. FRANK [*deliberately changing the conversation*]. I wonder where
Miep is. She's usually so prompt.

*Suddenly everything else is forgotten as they hear the sound of an
automobile coming to a screeching stop in the street below. They are
tense, motionless in their terror. The car starts away. A wave of
relief sweeps over them. They pick up their occupations again.* ANNE
flings open the door of PETER'S *room, making a dramatic entrance.
She is dressed in* PETER'S *clothes.* PETER *looks at her in fury. The
others are amused.*

5 ANNE. Good evening, everyone. Forgive me if I don't stay.
[*She jumps up on a chair.*] I have a friend waiting for me in
there. My friend Tom. Tom Cat. Some people say that
we look alike. But Tom has the most beautiful whiskers,
and I have only a little fuzz. I am hoping . . . in time . . .

6 PETER. All right, Mrs. Quack Quack!

7 ANNE [*outraged—jumping down*]. Peter!

8 PETER. I heard about you . . . How you talked so much in
class they called you Mrs. Quack Quack. How Mr.
Smitter made you write a composition . . . ' "Quack,
quack", said Mrs. Quack Quack.'

9 ANNE. Well, go on. Tell them the rest. How it was so good he
read it out loud to the class and then read it to all his
other classes!

10 PETER. Quack! Quack! Quack . . . Quack . . . Quack . . .

ANNE *pulls off the coat and trousers*

11 ANNE. You are the most intolerable, insufferable boy I've
ever met!

She throws the clothes down the stair-well. PETER *goes down after them.*

1   PETER. Quack, quack, quack!

2   MRS. VAN DAAN [*to* ANNE]. That's right, Anneke! Give it to him!

3   ANNE. With all the boys in the world . . . Why I had to get locked up with one like you! . . .

4   PETER. Quack, quack, quack, and from now on stay out of my room!

As PETER *passes her,* ANNE *puts out her foot, tripping him. He picks himself up, and goes on into his room.*

5   MRS. FRANK [*quietly*]. Anne, dear . . . your hair. [*She feels* ANNE'S *forehead.*] You're warm. Are you feeling all right?

6   ANNE. Please, Mother.

She goes over to the centre table, slipping into her shoes.

7   MRS. FRANK [*following her*]. You haven't a fever, have you?

8   ANNE [*pulling away*]. No. No.

9   MRS. FRANK. You know we can't call a doctor here, ever. There's only one thing to do . . . watch carefully. Prevent an illness before it comes. Let me see your tongue.

10   ANNE. Mother, this is perfectly absurd.

11   MRS. FRANK. Anne, dear, don't be such a baby. Let me see your tongue. [*As* ANNE *refuses,* MRS. FRANK *appeals to* MR. FRANK.] Otto . . . ?

12   MR. FRANK. You hear your mother, Anne.

ANNE *flicks out her tongue for a second, then turns away.*

13   MRS. FRANK. Come on—open up! [*as* ANNE *opens her mouth very wide*] You seem all right . . . but perhaps an aspirin . . .

1 MRS. VAN DAAN. For heaven's sake, don't give that child any pills. I waited for fifteen minutes this morning for her to come out of the W.C.

2 ANNE. I was washing my hair!

3 MR. FRANK. I think there's nothing the matter with our Anne that a ride on her bike, or a visit with her friend Jopie de Waal wouldn't cure. Isn't that so, Anne?

    MR. VAN DAAN *comes down into the room. From outside we hear faint sounds of bombers going over and a burst of ack-ack.*

4 MR. VAN DAAN. Miep not come yet?

5 MRS. VAN DAAN. The workmen just left, a little while ago.

6 MR. VAN DAAN. What's for dinner tonight?

7 MRS. VAN DAAN. Beans.

8 MR. VAN DAAN. Not again!

9 MRS. VAN DAAN. Poor Putti! I know. But what can we do? That's all that Miep brought us.

    MR. VAN DAAN *starts to pace, his hands behind his back.* ANNE *follows behind him, imitating him.*

10 ANNE. We are now in what is known as the 'bean cycle'. Beans boiled, beans en casserole, beans with strings, beans without strings . . .

    PETER *has come out of his room. He slides into his place at the table, becoming immediately absorbed in his studies.*

11 MR. VAN DAAN [*to* PETER]. I saw you . . . in there, playing with your cat.

12 MRS. VAN DAAN. He just went in for a second, putting his coat away. He's been out here all the time, doing his lessons.

13 MR. FRANK [*looking up from the papers*]. Anne, you got an excellent in your history paper today . . . and very good in Latin.

14 ANNE [*sitting beside him*]. How about algebra?

1 MR FRANK. I'll have to make a confession. Up until now I've managed to stay ahead of you in algebra. Today you caught up with me. We'll leave it to Margot to correct.

2 ANNE. Isn't algebra *vile*, Pim!

3 MR. FRANK. Vile!

4 MARGOT [*to* MR. FRANK]. How did I do?

5 ANNE [*getting up*]. Excellent, excellent, excellent, excellent!

6 MR. FRANK [*to* MARGOT]. You should have used the subjunctive here . . .

7 MARGOT. Should I? . . . I thought . . . look here . . . I didn't use it here . . .

The two become absorbed in the papers.

8 ANNE. Mrs. Van Daan, may I try on your coat?

9 MRS. FRANK. No, Anne.

10 MRS. VAN DAAN [*giving it to* ANNE]. It's all right . . . but careful with it. [ANNE *puts it on and struts with it.*] My father gave me that the year before he died. He always bought the best that money could buy.

11 ANNE. Mrs. Van Daan, did you have a lot of boy friends before you were married?

12 MRS. FRANK. Anne, that's a personal question. It's not courteous to ask personal questions.

13 MRS. VAN DAAN. Oh I don't mind. [*to* ANNE] Our house was always swarming with boys. When I was a girl we had . . .

14 MR. VAN DAAN. Oh, God. Not again!

15 MRS. VAN DAAN [*good-humoured*]. Shut up! [*without a pause, to* ANNE. MR. VAN DAAN *mimics* MRS. VAN DAAN, *speaking the first few words in unison with her*] One summer we had a big house in Hilversum. The boys came buzzing round like bees around a jam pot. And when I was sixteen! . . . We were wearing our skirts very short those days and I had good-looking legs. [*She pulls up her skirt, going to* MR. FRANK.] I

still have 'em. I may not be as pretty as I used to be, but I still have my legs. How about it, Mr. Frank?

2   MR. VAN DAAN. All right. All right. We see them.

3   MRS. VAN DAAN. I'm not asking you. I'm asking Mr. Frank.

4   PETER. Mother, for heaven's sake.

5   MRS. VAN DAAN. Oh, I embarrass you, do I? Well, I just hope the girl you marry has as good. [*Then to* ANNE.] My father used to worry about me, with so many boys hanging round. He told me, if any of them gets fresh, you say to him . . . 'Remember, Mr. So-and-So, remember I'm a lady'.

6   ANNE. 'Remember, Mr. So-and-So, remember I'm a lady.'

She gives MRS. VAN DAAN *her coat.*

7   MR. VAN DAAN. Look at you, talking that way in front of her! Don't you know she puts it all down in that diary?

8   MRS. VAN DAAN. So, if she does? I'm only telling the truth!

ANNE *stretches out, putting her ear to the floor, listening to what is going on below. The sound of the bombers fades away.*

9   MRS. FRANK [*setting the table*]. Would you mind, Peter, if I moved you over to the couch?

10   ANNE [*listening*]. Miep must have the radio on.

PETER *picks up his papers, going over to the couch beside* MRS. VAN DAAN.

11   MR. VAN DAAN [*accusingly, to* PETER]. Haven't you finished yet?

12   PETER. No.

13   MR. VAN DAAN. You ought to be ashamed of yourself.

14   PETER. All right. All right. I'm a dunce. I'm a hopeless case. Why do I go on?

15   MRS. VAN DAAN. You're not hopeless. Don't talk that way.

24

Suggested set design for The Diary of Anne Frank.

HEAVY ATTIC FLOOR CARRIED BY ROSTRUM OUTSIDE INTERIOR WALLS.

← TORMENTORS, MADE OF HEAVY RANNING AND SHAPED TO SUGGEST CEILING STRUCTURES. AIM TO CREATE A VISUAL PRESSURE WITHOUT CROWDING THE PLAYING SETTING.

Bill Prewes '69

The right side of the set showing Anne's room.

The left side of the set showing the stairs, stair-well and Peter's room.

THE BACK WALL OF ATTIC ROOM
LEFT OPEN AS A MEANS OF FLOODING
SET WITH BOMB ACTIVITY ETC. WITH
LIGHTING ALSO HELPING TO KEEP THE
SETTING OPEN WITHOUT DESTROYING THE
BASIC ATMOSPHER.

The attic room.

It's just that you haven't anyone to help you, like the girls have. [*To* MR. FRANK.] Maybe you could help him, Mr. Frank?

2   MR. FRANK. I'm sure that his father . . . ?

3   MR. VAN DAAN. Not me. I can't do anything with him. He won't listen to me. You go ahead . . . if you want.

4   MR. FRANK [*going to* PETER]. What about it, Peter? Shall we make our school co-educational?

5   MRS. VAN DAAN [*kissing* MR. FRANK]. You're an angel, Mr. Frank. An angel. I don't know why I didn't meet you before I met that one there. Here, sit down, Mr. Frank . . . [*She forces him down on the couch beside* PETER.] Now, Peter, you listen to Mr. Frank.

6   MR. FRANK. It might be better for us to go into Peter's room.

PETER *jumps up eagerly, leading the way.*

7   MRS. VAN DAAN. That's right. You go in there, Peter. You listen to Mr. Frank. Mr. Frank is a highly educated man.

As MR. FRANK *is about to follow* PETER *into his room,* MRS. FRANK *stops him and wipes the lipstick from his lips. Then she closes the door after them.*

8   ANNE [*on the floor, listening*]. Shh! I can hear a man's voice talking.

9   MR. VAN DAAN [*to* ANNE]. Isn't it bad enough here without your sprawling all over the place?

ANNE *sits up.*

10   MRS. VAN DAAN [*to* MR. VAN DAAN]. If you didn't smoke so much, you wouldn't be so bad-tempered.

11   MR. VAN DAAN. Am I smoking? Do you see me smoking?

12   MRS. VAN DAAN. Don't tell me you've used up all those cigarettes.

13   MR. VAN DAAN. One package. Miep only brought me one package.

25

1   MRS. VAN DAAN. It's a filthy habit anyway. It's a good time to break yourself.

2   MR. VAN DAAN. Oh, stop it, please.

3   MRS. VAN DAAN. You're smoking up all our money. You know that, don't you?

4   MR. VAN DAAN. Will you shut up? [*During this,* MRS. FRANK *and* MARGOT *have studiously kept their eyes down. But* ANNE, *seated on the floor, has been following the discussion interestedly.* MR. VAN DAAN *turns to see her staring up at him.*] And what are you staring at?

5   ANNE. I never heard grown-ups quarrel before. I thought only children quarrelled.

6   MR. VAN DAAN. This isn't a quarrel! It's a discussion. And I never heard children so rude before.

7   ANNE [*rising, indignantly*]. I, rude!

8   MR. VAN DAAN. Yes!

9   MRS. FRANK [*quickly*]. Anne, will you get me my knitting? [ANNE *goes to get it.*] I must remember, when Miep comes, to ask her to bring me some more wool.

10 MARGOT [*going to her room*]. I need some hairpins and some soap. I made a list.

    She goes into her bedroom to get the list.

11 MRS. FRANK [*to* ANNE]. Have you some library books for Miep when she comes?

12 ANNE. It's a wonder that Miep has a life of her own, the way we make her run errands for us. Please, Miep, get me some starch. Please take my hair out and have it cut. Tell me all the latest news, Miep. [*She goes over, kneeling on the couch beside* MRS. VAN DAAN.] Did you know she was engaged? His name is Dirk, and Miep's afraid the Nazis will ship him off to Germany to work in one of their war plants. That's what they're doing with some of the young Dutchmen . . . they pick them up off the streets—

1 MR. VAN DAAN [*interrupting*]. Don't you ever get tired of talk-ing? Suppose you try keeping still for five minutes. Just five minutes.

He starts to pace again. Again ANNE *follows him, mimicking him.* MRS. FRANK *jumps up and takes her by the arm up to the sink, and gives her a glass of milk.*

2 MRS. FRANK. Come here, Anne. It's time for your glass of milk.

3 MR. VAN DAAN. Talk, talk, talk. I never heard such a child. Where is my . . . ? Every evening it's the same, talk, talk, talk. [*He looks around.*] Where is my . . . ?

4 MRS. VAN DAAN. What're you looking for?

5 MR. VAN DAAN. My pipe. Have you seen my pipe?

6 MRS. VAN DAAN. What good's a pipe? You haven't got any tobacco.

7 MR. VAN DAAN. At least I'll have something to hold in my mouth! [*opening* MARGOT's *bedroom door*] Margot, have you seen my pipe?

8 MARGOT. It was on the table last night.

ANNE *puts her glass of milk on the table and picks up his pipe, hiding it behind her back.*

9 MR. VAN DAAN. I know. I know. Anne, did you see my pipe? . . . Anne!

10 MRS. FRANK. Anne, Mr. Van Daan is speaking to you.

11 ANNE. Am I allowed to talk now?

12 MR. VAN DAAN. You're the most aggravating . . . The trouble with you is, you've been spoiled. What you need is a good old-fashioned spanking.

13 ANNE [*mimicking* MRS. VAN DAAN]. 'Remember, Mr. So-and-So, remember I'm a lady.'

27

She thrusts the pipe into his mouth, then picks up her glass of milk.
MARGOT *comes out of the bedroom and places the list on the table.*

1   MR. VAN DAAN [*restraining himself with difficulty*]. Why aren't you nice and quiet like your sister Margot? Why do you have to show off all the time? Let me give you a little advice, young lady. Men don't like that kind of thing in a girl. You know that? A man likes a girl who'll listen to him once in a while ... a domestic girl, who'll keep her house shining for her husband ... who loves to cook and sew and ...

2   ANNE. I'd cut my throat first! I'd open my veins! I'm going to be remarkable! I'm going to Paris ...

3   MR. VAN DAAN [*scoffingly*]. Paris!

4   ANNE. ... to study music and art.

5   MR. VAN DAAN. Yeah! Yeah!

6   ANNE. I'm going to be a famous dancer or singer ... or something wonderful.

She makes a wide gesture, spilling the glass of milk on the fur coat in MRS. VAN DAAN'S *lap.* MARGOT *rushes quickly over with a towel.* ANNE *tries to brush the milk off with her skirt.*

7   MRS. VAN DAAN. Now look what you've done ... you clumsy little fool! My beautiful fur coat my father gave me ...

8   ANNE. I'm so sorry.

9   MRS. VAN DAAN. What do you care? It isn't yours ... So go on, ruin it! Do you know what that coat cost? Do you? And now look at it! Look at it!

10   ANNE. I'm very, very sorry.

11   MRS. VAN DAAN. I could kill you for this. I could just kill you!

MRS. VAN DAAN *goes up the stairs, clutching the coat.* MR. VAN DAAN *starts after her.*

12   MR. VAN DAAN. Petronella ... *liefje! Liefje!* ... Come back ... the supper ... come back!

13   MRS. FRANK. Anne, you must not behave in that way.

1   ANNE. It was an accident. Anyone can have an accident.

2   MRS. FRANK. I don't mean that. I mean the answering back. You must not answer back. They are our guests. We must always show the greatest courtesy to them. We're all living under terrible tension. [*She stops as* MARGOT *indicates that* VAN DAAN *can hear. When he is gone, she continues.*] That's why we must control ourselves . . . You don't hear Margot getting into arguments with them, do you? Watch Margot. She's always courteous with them. Never familiar. She keeps her distance. And they respect her for it. Try to be like Margot.

3   ANNE. And have them walk all over me, the way they do her? No, thanks!

4   MRS. FRANK. I'm not afraid that anyone is going to walk all over you, Anne. I'm afraid for other people, that you'll walk on them. I don't know what happens to you, Anne. You are wild, self-willed. If I had ever talked to my mother as you talk to me . . .

5   ANNE. Things have changed. People aren't like that any more. 'Yes, Mother.' 'No, Mother.' 'Anything you say, Mother.' I've got to fight things out for myself! Make something of myself!

6   MRS. FRANK. It isn't necessary to fight to do it. Margot doesn't fight, and isn't she . . . ?

7   ANNE [*violently rebellious*]. Margot! Margot! Margot! That's all I hear from everyone . . . how wonderful Margot is . . . 'Why aren't you like Margot?'

8   MARGOT [*protesting*]. Oh, come on, Anne, don't be so . . .

9   ANNE [*paying no attention*]. Everything she does is right, and everything I do is wrong! I'm the goat around here! . . . You're all against me! . . . And you worst of all!

She rushes off into her room and throws herself down on the couch, stifling her sobs. MRS. FRANK *sighs and starts towards the stove.*

1   MRS. FRANK [*to* MARGOT]. Let's put the soup on the stove . . .
    if there's anyone who cares to eat. Margot, will you take
    the bread out? [MARGOT *gets the bread from the cupboard.*] I
    don't know how we can go on living this way . . . I can't
    say a word to Anne . . . she flies at me . . .

2   MARGOT. You know Anne. In half an hour she'll be out
    here, laughing and joking.

3   MRS. FRANK. And . . . [*She makes a motion upwards, indicating the*
    VAN DAANS.] . . . I told your father it wouldn't work . . .
    but no . . . no . . . he had to ask them, he said . . . he
    owed it to him, he said. Well, he knows now that I was
    right! These quarrels! . . . This bickering!

4   MARGOT [*with a warning look*]. Shush. Shush.

    The buzzer for the door sounds. MRS. FRANK *gasps, startled.*

5   MRS. FRANK. Every time I hear that sound, my heart stops!

6   MARGOT [*starting for* PETER'S *door*]. It's Miep. [*She knocks at the*
    door.] Father?

    MR. FRANK *comes quickly from* PETER'S *room.*

7   MR. FRANK. Thank you, Margot. [*As he goes down the steps to open*
    the outer door.] Has everyone his list?

8   MARGOT. I'll get my books. [*giving her mother a list*] Here's your
    list. [MARGOT *goes into her and* ANNE'S *bedroom on the right.*
    ANNE *sits up, hiding her tears, as* MARGOT *comes in.*] Miep's here.

    MARGOT *picks up her books and goes back.* ANNE *hurries over to the*
    mirror, smoothing her hair.

9   MR. VAN DAAN [*coming down the stairs*]. Is it Miep?

10 MARGOT. Yes, Father's gone down to let her in.

11 MR. VAN DAAN. At last I'll have some cigarettes!

12 MRS. FRANK [*to* MR. VAN DAAN]. I can't tell you how unhappy
    I am about Mrs. Van Daan's coat. Anne should never
    have touched it.

1 MR. VAN DAAN. She'll be all right.

2 MRS. FRANK. Is there anything I can do?

3 MR. VAN DAAN. Don't worry.

He turns to meet MIEP. *But it is not* MIEP *who comes up the steps. It is* MR. KRALER, *followed by* MR. FRANK. *Their faces are grave.* ANNE *comes from the bedroom.* PETER *comes from his room.*

4 MRS. FRANK. Mr. Kraler!

5 MR. VAN DAAN. How are you, Mr. Kraler?

6 MARGOT. This is a surprise.

7 MRS. FRANK. When Mr. Kraler comes, the sun begins to shine.

8 MR. VAN DAAN. Miep is coming?

9 MR. KRALER. Not tonight.

KRALER *goes to* MARGOT *and* MRS. FRANK *and* ANNE, *shaking hands with them.*

10 MRS. FRANK. Wouldn't you like a cup of coffee? . . . Or, better still, will you have supper with us?

11 MR. FRANK. Mr. Kraler has something to talk over with us. Something has happened, he says, which demands an immediate decision.

12 MRS. FRANK [*fearful*]. What is it?

MR. KRALER *sits down on the couch. As he talks he takes bread, cabbages, milk, etc., from his briefcase, giving them to* MARGOT *and* ANNE *to put away.*

13 MR. KRALER. Usually, when I come up here, I try to bring you some bit of good news. What's the use of telling you the bad news when there's nothing that you can do about it? But today something has happened . . . Dirk . . . Miep's Dirk, you know, came to me just now. He tells me that he has a Jewish friend living near him. A dentist. He says he's in trouble. He begged me, could I do anything for this man? Could I find him a hiding place? . . .

31

So I've come to you . . . I know it's a terrible thing to ask of you, living as you are, but would you take him in with you?

2   MR. FRANK. Of course we will.

3   MR. KRALER [*rising*]. It'll be just for a night or two . . . until I find some other place. This happened so suddenly that I didn't know where to turn.

4   MR. FRANK. Where is he?

5   MR. KRALER. Downstairs in the office.

6   MR. FRANK. Good. Bring him up.

7   MR. KRALER. His name is Dussel . . . Jan Dussel.

8   MR. FRANK. Dussel . . . I think I know him.

9   MR. KRALER. I'll get him.

He goes quickly down the steps and out. MR. FRANK *suddenly becomes conscious of the others.*

10   MR. FRANK. Forgive me. I spoke without consulting you. But I knew you'd feel as I do.

11   MR. VAN DAAN. There's no reason for you to consult anyone. This is your place. You have a right to do exactly as you please. The only thing I feel . . . there's so little food as it is . . . and to take in another person . . .

PETER *turns away, ashamed of his father.*

12   MR. FRANK. We can stretch the food a little. It's only for a few days.

13   MR. VAN DAAN. You want to make a bet?

14   MRS. FRANK. I think it's fine to have him. But, Otto, where are you going to put him? Where?

15   PETER. He can have my bed. I can sleep on the floor. I wouldn't mind.

16   MR. FRANK. That's good of you, Peter. But your room's too small . . . even for *you.*

1   ANNE. I have a much better idea. I'll come in here with you and Mother, and Margot can take Peter's room and Peter can go in our room with Mr. Dussel.

2   MARGOT. That's right. We could do that.

3   MR. FRANK. No, Margot. You mustn't sleep in that room . . . neither you nor Anne. Mouschi has caught some rats in there. Peter's brave. He doesn't mind.

4   ANNE. Then how about *this*? I'll come in here with you and Mother, and Mr. Dussel can have my bed.

5   MRS. FRANK. No. No. *No!* Margot will come in here with us and he can have her bed. It's the only way. Margot, bring your things in here. Help her, Anne.

MARGOT hurries into her room to get her things.

6   ANNE [*to her mother*]. Why Margot? Why can't I come in here?

7   MRS. FRANK. Because it wouldn't be proper for Margot to sleep with a . . . Please, Anne. Don't argue. Please.

ANNE starts slowly away.

8   MR. FRANK [*to* ANNE]. You don't mind sharing your room with Mr. Dussel, do you, Anne?

9   ANNE. No. No, of course not.

10 MR. FRANK. Good. [ANNE *goes off into her bedroom, helping* MARGOT. MR. FRANK *starts to search in the cupboards.*] Where's the cognac?

11 MRS. FRANK. It's there. But, Otto, I was saving it in case of illness.

12 MR. FRANK. I think we couldn't find a better time to use it. Peter, will you get five glasses for me?

PETER goes for the glasses. MARGOT comes out of her bedroom, carrying her possessions, which she hangs behind a curtain in the main room. MR. FRANK finds the cognac and pours it into the five glasses that PETER brings him. MR. VAN DAAN stands looking on sourly. MRS. VAN DAAN comes downstairs and looks around at all the bustle.

33

D

1 MRS. VAN DAAN. What's happening? What's going on?

2 MR. VAN DAAN. Someone's moving in with us.

3 MRS. VAN DAAN. In here? You're joking.

4 MARGOT. It's only for a night or two . . . until Mr. Kraler finds him another place.

5 MR. VAN DAAN. Yeah! Yeah!

> MR. FRANK *hurries over as* MR. KRALER *and* DUSSEL *come up.* DUSSEL *is a man in his late fifties, meticulous, finicky . . . bewildered now. He wears a raincoat. He carries a briefcase, stuffed full, and a small medicine case.*

6 MR. FRANK. Come in, Mr. Dussel.

7 MR. KRALER. This is Mr. Frank.

8 DUSSEL. Mr. Otto Frank?

9 MR. FRANK. Yes. Let me take your things. [*He takes the hat and briefcase, but* DUSSEL *clings to his medicine case.*] This is my wife Edith . . . Mr. and Mrs. Van Daan . . . their son, Peter . . . and my daughters, Margot and Anne.

> DUSSEL *shakes hands with everyone.*

10 MR. KRALER. Thank you, Mr. Frank. Thank you all. Mr. Dussel, I leave you in good hands. Oh . . . Dirk's coat.

> DUSSEL *hurriedly takes off the raincoat, giving it to* MR. KRALER. *Underneath is his white dentist's jacket, with a yellow Star of David on it.*

11 DUSSEL [*to* MR. KRALER]. What can I say to thank you . . . ?

12 MRS. FRANK [*to* DUSSEL]. Mr. Kraler and Miep . . . They're our life line. Without them we couldn't live.

13 MR. KRALER. Please. Please. You make us seem very heroic. It isn't that at all. We simply don't like the Nazis. [*to* MR. FRANK, *who offers him a drink*] No, thanks. [*then going on*] We don't like their methods. We don't like . . .

34

1   MR. FRANK [*smiling*]. I know. I know. 'No one's going to tell us Dutchmen what to do with our damn Jews!'

2   MR. KRALER [*to* DUSSEL]. Pay no attention to Mr. Frank. I'll be up tomorrow to see that they're treating you right. [*to* MR. FRANK] Don't trouble to come down again. Peter will bolt the door after me, won't you, Peter?

3   PETER. Yes, sir.

4   MR. FRANK. Thank you, Peter. I'll do it.

5   MR. KRALER. Good night. Good night.

6   GROUP. Good night, Mr. Kraler. We'll see you tomorrow, etc., etc.

> MR. KRALER *goes out with* MR. FRANK. MRS. FRANK *gives each one of the 'grown-ups' a glass of cognac.*

7   MRS. FRANK. Please, Mr. Dussel, sit down.

> MR. DUSSEL *sinks into a chair.* MRS. FRANK *gives him a glass of cognac.*

8   DUSSEL. I'm dreaming. I know it. I can't believe my eyes. Mr. Otto Frank here! [*to* MRS. FRANK] You're not in Switzerland then? A woman told me . . . She said she'd gone to your house . . . the door was open, everything was in disorder, dishes in the sink. She said she found a piece of paper in the wastebasket with an address scribbled on it . . . an address in Zurich. She said you must have escaped to Zurich.

9   ANNE. Father put that there purposely . . . just so people would think that very thing!

10 DUSSEL. And you've been *here* all the time?

11 MRS. FRANK. All the time . . . ever since July.

> ANNE *speaks to her father as he comes back.*

12 ANNE. It worked, Pim . . . the address you left! Mr. Dussel says that people believe we escaped to Switzerland.

1   MR. FRANK. I'm glad ... And now let's have a little drink to welcome Mr. Dussel. [*Before they can drink,* MR. DUSSEL *bolts his drink.* MR. FRANK *smiles and raises his glass.*] To Mr. Dussel. Welcome. We're very honoured to have you with us.

2   MRS. FRANK. To Mr. Dussel, welcome.

The VAN DAAN'S *murmur a welcome. The 'grown-ups' drink.*

3   MRS. VAN DAAN. Um. That was good.

4   MR. VAN DAAN. Did Mr. Kraler warn you that you won't get much to eat here? You can imagine ... three ration books among the seven of us ... and now you make eight.

PETER *walks away, humiliated. Outside a street organ is heard dimly.*

5   DUSSEL [*rising*]. Mr. Van Daan, you don't realize what is happening outside that you should warn me of a thing like that. You don't realize what's going on ... [*As* MR. VAN DAAN *starts his characteristic pacing,* DUSSEL *turns to speak to the others.*] Right here in Amsterdam every day hundreds of Jews disappear ... They surround a block and search house by house. Children come home from school to find their parents gone. Hundreds are being deported ... people that you and I know ... the Hallensteins ... the Wessels ...

6   MRS. FRANK [*in tears*]. Oh, no. No!

7   DUSSEL. They get their call-up notice ... come to the Jewish theatre on such and such a day and hour ... bring only what you can carry in a rucksack. And if you refuse the call-up notice, then they come and drag you from home and ship you off to Mauthausen. The death camp!

8   MRS. FRANK. We didn't know that things had got so much worse.

9   DUSSEL. Forgive me for speaking so.

36

1 ANNE [*coming to* DUSSEL]. Do you know the de Waals? . . . What's become of them? Their daughter Jopie and I are in the same class. Jopie's my best friend.

2 DUSSEL. They are gone.

3 ANNE. Gone?

4 DUSSEL. With all the others.

5 ANNE. Oh, no. Not Jopie!

She turns away, in tears. MRS. FRANK *motions to* MARGOT *to comfort her.* MARGOT *goes to* ANNE, *putting her arms comfortingly around her.*

6 MRS. VAN DAAN. There were some people called Wagner. They lived near us . . . ?

7 MR. FRANK [*interrupting, with a glance at* ANNE). I think we should put this off until later. We all have many questions we want to ask . . . But I'm sure that Mr. Dussel would like to get settled before supper.

8 DUSSEL. Thank you. I would. I brought very little with me.

9 MR. FRANK [*giving him his hat and briefcase*]. I'm sorry we can't give you a room alone. But I hope you won't be too uncomfortable. We've had to make strict rules here . . . a schedule of hours . . . We'll tell you after supper. Anne, would you like to take Mr. Dussel to his room?

10 ANNE [*controlling her tears*]. If you'll come with me, Mr. Dussel?

She starts for her room.

11 DUSSEL [*shaking hands with each in turn*]. Forgive me if I haven't really expressed my gratitude to all of you. This has been such a shock to me. I'd always thought of myself as Dutch. I was born in Holland. My father was born in Holland, and my grandfather. And now . . . after all these years . . . [*He breaks off.*] If you'll excuse me.

DUSSEL *gives a little bow and hurries off after* ANNE. MR. FRANK *and the others are subdued.*

37

1   ANNE [*turning on the light*]. Well, here we are.

> DUSSEL *looks around the room. In the main room* MARGOT *speaks to her mother.*

2   MARGOT. The news sounds pretty bad, doesn't it? It's so different from what Mr. Kraler tells us. Mr. Kraler says things are improving.

3   MR. VAN DAAN. I like it better the way Kraler tells it.

> *They resume their occupations, quietly.* PETER *goes off into his room. In* ANNE'S *room,* ANNE *turns to* DUSSEL.

4   ANNE. You're going to share the room with me.

5   DUSSEL. I'm a man who's always lived alone. I haven't had to adjust myself to others. I hope you'll bear with me until I learn.

6   ANNE. Let me help you. [*She takes his briefcase.*] Do you always live all alone? Have you no family at all?

7   DUSSEL. No one.

> *He opens his medicine case and spreads his bottles on the dressing table.*

8   ANNE. How dreadful. You must be terribly lonely.

9   DUSSEL. I'm used to it.

10 ANNE. I don't think I could ever get used to it. Didn't you even have a pet? A cat, or a dog?

11 DUSSEL. I have an allergy for fur-bearing animals. They give me asthma.

12 ANNE. Oh, dear. Peter has a cat.

13 DUSSEL. Here? He has it here?

14 ANNE. Yes. But we hardly ever see it. He keeps it in his room all the time. I'm sure it will be all right.

15 DUSSEL. Let us hope so.

> *He takes some pills to fortify himself.*

1   ANNE. That's Margot's bed, where you're going to sleep. I
    sleep on the sofa there. [*indicating the clothes hooks on the wall*]
    We cleared these off for your things. [*She goes over to the
    window.*] The best part about this room . . . you can look
    down and see a bit of the street and the canal. There's a
    houseboat . . . you can see the end of it . . . a bargeman
    lives there with his family . . . They have a baby and he's
    just beginning to walk and I'm so afraid he's going to
    fall into the canal some day. I watch him. . . .

2   DUSSEL [*interrupting*]. Your father spoke of a schedule.

3   ANNE [*coming away from the window*]. Oh, yes. It's mostly about the
    times we have to be quiet. And times for the W.C. You
    can use it now if you like.

4   DUSSEL [*stiffly*]. No, thank you.

5   ANNE. I suppose you think it's awful, my talking about a
    thing like that. But you don't know how important it
    can get to be, especially when you're frightened . . .
    About this room, the way Margot and I did . . . she had
    it to herself in the afternoons for studying, reading . . .
    lessons, you know . . . and I took the mornings. Would
    that be all right with you?

6   DUSSEL. I'm not at my best in the morning.

7   ANNE. You stay here in the mornings then. I'll take the room
    in the afternoons.

8   DUSSEL. Tell me, when you're in here, what happens to me?
    Where am I spending my time? In there, with all the
    people?

9   ANNE. Yes.

10 DUSSEL. I see. I see.

11 ANNE. We have supper at half past six.

12 DUSSEL [*going over to the sofa*]. Then, if you don't mind . . . I like
    to lie down quietly for ten minutes before eating. I
    find it helps the digestion.

39

1   ANNE. Of course. I hope I'm not going to be too much of a bother to you. I seem to be able to get everyone's back up.

DUSSEL lies down on the sofa, curled up, his back to her.

2   DUSSEL. I always get along very well with children. My patients all bring their children to me, because they know I get on well with them. So don't you worry about that.

ANNE leans over him, taking his hand and shaking it gratefully.

3   ANNE. Thank you. Thank you, Mr. Dussel.

The lights dim to darkness. The curtain falls on the scene. ANNE'S VOICE *comes to us faintly at first, and then with increasing power.*

4   ANNE'S VOICE. . . . And yesterday I finished Cissy Van Marxvelt's latest book. I think she is a first-class writer. I shall definitely let my children read her. Monday the twenty-first of September, nineteen forty-two. Mr. Dussel and I had another battle yesterday. Yes, Mr. Dussel! According to him, nothing, I repeat . . . nothing, is right about me . . . my appearance, my character, my manners. While he was going on at me I thought . . . sometime I'll give you such a smack that you'll fly right up to the ceiling! Why is it that every grown-up thinks he knows the way to bring up children? Particularly the grown-ups that never had any. I keep wishing that Peter was a girl instead of a boy. Then I would have someone to talk to. Margot's a darling, but she takes everything too seriously. To pause for a moment on the subject of Mrs. Van Daan. I must tell you that her attempts to flirt with Father are getting her nowhere. Pim, thank goodness, won't play.

As she is saying the last lines, the curtain rises on the darkened scene. ANNE'S VOICE *fades out.*

SCENE 4

It is the middle of the night, several months later. The stage is dark except for a little light which comes through the skylight in PETER'S *room.*

Everyone is in bed. MR. *and* MRS. FRANK *lie on the couch in the main room, which has been pulled out to serve as a makeshift double bed.*

MARGOT *is sleeping on a mattress on the floor in the main room, behind a curtain stretched across for privacy. The others are all in their accustomed rooms.*

From outside we hear two drunken soldiers singing 'Lili Marlene'. A girl's high giggle is heard. The sound of running feet is heard coming closer and then fading in the distance. Throughout the scene there is the distant sound of aeroplanes passing overhead.

A match suddenly flares up in the attic. We dimly see MR. VAN DAAN. *He is getting his bearings. He comes quickly down the stairs, and goes to the cupboard where the food is stored. Again the match flares up, and is as quickly blown out. The dim figure is seen to steal back up the stairs.*

There is quiet for a second or two, broken only by the sound of aeroplanes, and running feet on the street below.

Suddenly, out of the silence and the dark, we hear ANNE *scream.*

1   ANNE [*screaming*]. No! No! Don't . . . don't take me!

> *She moans, tossing and crying in her sleep. The other people wake, terrified.* DUSSEL *sits up in bed, furious.*

2   DUSSEL. Shush! Anne! Anne, for God's sake, shush!

3   ANNE [*still in her nightmare*]. Save me! Save me!

> *She screams and screams.* DUSSEL *gets out of bed, going over to her, trying to wake her.*

4   DUSSEL. For God's sake! Quiet! Quiet! You want someone to hear?

> *In the main room* MRS. FRANK *grabs a shawl and pulls it around her. She rushes in to* ANNE, *taking her in her arms.* MR. FRANK *hurriedly gets up, putting on his overcoat.* MARGOT *sits up, terrified.* PETER'S *light goes on in his room.*

5   MRS. FRANK [*to* ANNE, *in her room*]. Hush, darling, hush. It's all right. [*over her shoulder to* DUSSEL] Will you be kind enough

41

to turn on the light, Mr. Dussel? [*back to* ANNE] It's nothing, my darling. It was just a dream.

DUSSEL *turns on the light in the bedroom.* MRS. FRANK *holds* ANNE *in her arms. Gradually* ANNE *comes out of her nightmare, still trembling with horror.* MR. FRANK *comes into the room, and goes quickly to the window, looking out to be sure that no one outside has heard* ANNE'S *screams.* MRS. FRANK *holds* ANNE, *talking softly to her. In the main room* MARGOT *stands on a chair, turning on the centre hanging lamp. A light goes on in the* VAN DAANS' *room overhead.* PETER *puts his robe on, coming out of his room.*

2 DUSSEL [*to* MRS. FRANK, *blowing his nose*]. Something must be done about that child, Mrs. Frank. Yelling like that! Who knows but there's somebody on the streets? She's endangering our lives.

3 MRS. FRANK. Anne, darling.

4 DUSSEL. Every night she twists and turns. I don't sleep. I spend half my night shushing her. And now it's nightmares!

MARGOT *comes to the door of* ANNE'S *room, followed by* PETER. MR. FRANK *goes to them, indicating that everything is all right.* PETER *takes* MARGOT *back.*

5 MRS. FRANK [*to* ANNE]. You're here, safe, you see? Nothing has happened. [*to* DUSSEL] Please, Mr. Dussel, go back to bed. She'll be herself in a minute or two. Won't you, Anne?

6 DUSSEL [*picking up a book and a pillow*]. Thank you, but I'm going to the W.C. The one place where there's peace!

He *stalks out.* MR. VAN DAAN, *in underwear and trousers, comes down the stairs.*

7 MR. VAN DAAN [*to* DUSSEL]. What is it? What happened?

8 DUSSEL. A nightmare. She was having a nightmare!

9 MR. VAN DAAN. I thought someone was murdering her.

10 DUSSEL. Unfortunately, no.

He goes into the bathroom. MR. VAN DAAN *goes back up the stairs.* MR. FRANK, *in the main room, sends* PETER *back to his own bedroom.*

1 MR. FRANK. Thank you, Peter. Go back to bed.

> PETER *goes back to his room.* MR. FRANK *follows him, turning out the light and looking out the window. Then he goes back to the main room, and gets up on a chair, turning out the centre hanging lamp.*

2 MRS. FRANK [*to* ANNE]. Would you like some water? [ANNE *shakes her head.*] Was it a very bad dream? Perhaps if you told me . . . ?

3 ANNE. I'd rather not talk about it.

4 MRS. FRANK. Poor darling. Try to sleep then. I'll sit right here beside you until you fall asleep.

> *She brings a stool over, sitting there.*

5 ANNE. You don't have to.

6 MRS. FRANK. But I'd like to stay with you . . . very much. Really.

7 ANNE. I'd rather you didn't.

8 MRS. FRANK. Good night, then. [*She leans down to kiss* ANNE. ANNE *throws her arm up over her face, turning away.* MRS. FRANK, *hiding her hurt, kisses* ANNE'S *arm.*] You'll be all right? There's nothing that you want?

9 ANNE. Will you please ask Father to come.

10 MRS. FRANK [*after a second*]. Of course, Anne dear. [*She hurries out into the other room.* MR. FRANK *comes to her as she comes in.*] Sie verlangt nach Dir!

11 MR. FRANK [*sensing her hurt*]. Edith, Liebe, schau . . .

12 MRS. FRANK. Es macht nichts! Ich danke dem lieben Herrgott, dass sie sich wenigstens an Dich wendet, wenn sie Trost braucht! Geh hinein, Otto, sie ist ganz hysterisch vor Angst. [*As* MR. FRANK *hesitates.*] Geh zu ihr. [*He looks at her for a second and then goes to get a cup of water for* ANNE. MRS. FRANK *sinks down on the bed, her face in her hands, trying to keep*

43

from sobbing aloud. MARGOT *comes over to her, putting her arms around her.*] She wants nothing of me. She pulled away when I leaned down to kiss her.

2 MARGOT. It's a phase ... You heard Father ... Most girls go through it ... they turn to their fathers at this age ... they give all their love to their fathers.

3 MRS. FRANK. You weren't like this. You didn't shut me out.

4 MARGOT. She'll get over it ...

She smooths the bed for MRS. FRANK *and sits beside her a moment as* MRS. FRANK *lies down. In* ANNE'S *room* MR. FRANK *comes in, sitting down by* ANNE. ANNE *flings her arms around him, clinging to him. In the distance we hear the sound of ack-ack.*

5 ANNE. Oh, Pim. I dreamed that they came to get us! The Green Police! They broke down the door and grabbed me and started to drag me out the way they did Jopie.

6 MR. FRANK. I want you to take this pill.

7 ANNE. What is it?

8 MR. FRANK. Something to quiet you.

She takes it and drinks the water. In the main room MARGOT *turns out the light and goes back to her bed.*

9 MR. FRANK [*to* ANNE]. Do you want me to read to you for a while?

10 ANNE. No. Just sit with me for a minute. Was I awful? Did I yell terribly loud? Do you think anyone outside could have heard?

11 MR. FRANK. No. No. Lie quietly now. Try to sleep.

12 ANNE. I'm a terrible coward. I'm so disappointed in myself. I think I've conquered my fear ... I think I'm really grown-up ... and then something happens ... and I run to you like a baby ... I love you, Father. I don't love anyone but you.

13 MR. FRANK [*reproachfully*]. Annele!

44

1 ANNE. It's true. I've been thinking about it for a long time. You're the only one I love.

2 MR. FRANK. It's fine to hear you tell me that you love me. But I'd be happier if you said you loved your mother as well . . . She needs your help so much . . . your love . . .

3 ANNE. We have nothing in common. She doesn't understand me. Whenever I try to explain my views on life to her she asks me if I'm constipated.

4 MR. FRANK. You hurt her very much just now. She's crying. She's in there crying.

5 ANNE. I can't help it. I only told the truth. I didn't want her here . . . *[then, with sudden change]* Oh, Pim, I was horrible, wasn't I? And the worst of it is, I can stand off and look at myself doing it and know it's cruel and yet I can't stop doing it. What's the matter with me? Tell me. Don't say it's just a phase! Help me.

6 MR. FRANK. There is so little that we parents can do to help our children. We can only try to set a good example . . . point the way. The rest you must do yourself. You must build your own character.

7 ANNE. I'm trying. Really I am. Every night I think back over all of the things I did that day that were wrong . . . like putting the wet mop in Mr. Dussel's bed . . . and this thing now with Mother. I say to myself, that was wrong. I make up my mind, I'm never going to do that again. Never! Of course I may do something worse . . . but at least I'll never do *that* again! . . . I have a nicer side, Father . . . a sweeter, nicer side. But I'm scared to show it. I'm afraid that people are going to laugh at me if I'm serious. So the mean Anne comes to the outside and the good Anne stays on the inside, and I keep on trying to switch them around and have the good Anne outside and the bad Anne inside and be what I'd like to be . . . and might be . . . if only . . . only . . .

She is asleep. MR. FRANK *watches her for a moment and then turns*

45

*off the light, and starts out. The lights dim out. The curtain falls on
the scene.* ANNE'S VOICE *is heard dimly at first, and then with
growing strength.*

1 ANNE'S VOICE. . . . The air-raids are getting worse. They come
over day and night. The noise is terrifying. Pim says it
should be music to our ears. The more planes, the
sooner will come the end of the war. Mrs. Van Daan
pretends to be a fatalist. What will be, will be. But when
the planes come over, who is the most frightened?
No one else but Petronella! . . . Monday, the ninth of
November, nineteen forty-two. Wonderful news! The
Allies have landed in Africa. Pim says that we can look
for an early finish to the war. Just for fun he asked each
of us what was the first thing we wanted to do when we
got out of here. Mrs. Van Daan longs to be home with
her own things, her needle-point chairs, the Beckstein
piano her father gave her . . . the best that money could
buy. Peter would like to go to a film. Mr. Dussel
wants to get back to his dentist's drill. He's afraid he is
losing his touch. For myself, there are so many things
. . . to ride a bike again . . . to laugh till my belly aches . . .
to have new clothes from the skin out . . . to have a hot
tub filled to overflowing and wallow in it for hours . . .
to be back in school with my friends . . .

*As the last lines are being said, the curtain rises on the scene. The
lights dim on as* ANNE'S VOICE *fades away.*

SCENE 5

It is the first night of the Hanukkah celebration. MR. FRANK *is standing at the
head of the table on which is the Menorah. He lights the Shamos, or servant
candle, and holds it as he says the blessing. Seated listening is all of the 'family',
dressed in their best. The men wear hats,* PETER *wears his cap.*

2 MR. FRANK [*reading from a prayer book*]. 'Praised be Thou, oh Lord
our God, Ruler of the universe, who has sanctified us

with Thy commandments and bidden us kindle the Hanukkah lights. Praised be Thou, oh Lord our God, Ruler of the universe, who has wrought wondrous deliverances for our fathers in days of old. Praised be Thou, oh Lord our God, Ruler of the universe, that Thou has given us life and sustenance and brought us to this happy season.' [MR. FRANK *lights the one candle of the Menorah as he continues*] 'We kindle this Hanukkah light to celebrate the great and wonderful deeds wrought through the zeal with which God filled the hearts of the heroic Maccabees, two thousand years ago. They fought against indifference, against tyranny and oppression, and they restored our Temple to us. May these lights remind us that we should ever look to God, whence cometh our help.' Amen.

2 ALL. Amen.

    MR. FRANK *hands* MRS. FRANK *the prayer book.*

3 MRS. FRANK [*reading*]. 'I lift up mine eyes unto the mountains, from whence cometh my help. My help cometh from the Lord who made heaven and earth. He will not suffer thy foot to be moved. He that keepeth thee will not slumber. He that keepeth Israel doth neither slumber nor sleep. The Lord is thy keeper. The Lord is thy shade upon thy right hand. The sun shall not smite thee by day, nor the moon by night. The Lord shall keep thee from all evil. He shall keep thy soul. The Lord shall guard thy going out and thy coming in, from this time forth and for evermore.' Amen.

4 ALL. Amen.

    MRS. FRANK *puts down the prayer book and goes to get the food and wine.* MARGOT *helps her.* MR. FRANK *takes the men's hats and puts them aside.*

5 DUSSEL [*rising*]. That was very moving.

6 ANNE [*pulling him back*]. It isn't over yet!

7 MRS. VAN DAAN. Sit down! Sit down!

1   ANNE. There's a lot more, songs and presents.

2   DUSSEL. Presents?

3   MRS. FRANK. Not this year, unfortunately.

4   MRS. VAN DAAN. But always on Hanukkah everyone gives presents . . . everyone!

5   DUSSEL. Like our St. Nicholas' Day.

There is a chorus of 'no's' from the group.

6   MRS. VAN DAAN. No! Not like St. Nicholas! What kind of a Jew are you that you don't know Hanukkah?

7   MRS. FRANK [*as she brings the food*]. I remember particularly the candles . . . First one, as we have tonight. Then the second night you light two candles, the next night three . . . and so on until you have eight candles burning. When there are eight candles it is truly beautiful.

8   MRS. VAN DAAN. And the potato pancakes.

9   MR. VAN DAAN. Don't talk about them!

10   MRS. VAN DAAN. I make the best *latkes* you ever tasted!

11   MRS. FRANK. Invite us all next year . . . in your own home.

12   MR. FRANK. God willing!

13   MRS. VAN DAAN. God willing.

14   MARGOT. What I remember best is the presents we used to get when we were little . . . eight days of presents . . . and each day they got better and better.

15   MRS. FRANK [*sitting down*]. We are all here, alive. That is present enough.

16   ANNE. No, it isn't. I've got something . . .

She rushes into her room, hurriedly puts on a little hat improvised from the lamp shade, grabs a satchel bulging with parcels and comes running back.

17   MRS. FRANK. What is it?

1   ANNE. Presents!

2   MRS. VAN DAAN. Presents!

3   DUSSEL. Look!

4   MR. VAN DAAN. What's she got on her head?

5   PETER. A lamp shade!

6   ANNE [*she picks out one at random*]. This is for Margot. [*She hands it to* MARGOT, *pulling her to her feet.*] Read it out loud.

7   MARGOT [*reading*]. 'You have never lost your temper.
    You never will, I fear,
    You are so good.
    But if you should,
    Put all your cross words here.'

    She tears open the package.

    A new crossword puzzle book! Where did you get it?

8   ANNE. It isn't new. It's one that you've done. But I rubbed it all out, and if you wait a little and forget, you can do it all over again.

9   MARGOT [*sitting*]. It's wonderful, Anne. Thank you. You'd never know it wasn't new.

    From outside we hear the sound of a streetcar passing.

10 ANNE [*with another gift*]. Mrs. Van Daan.

11 MRS. VAN DAAN [*taking it*]. This is awful . . . I haven't anything for anyone . . . I never thought . . .

12 MR. FRANK. This is all Anne's idea.

13 MRS. VAN DAAN [*holding up a bottle*]. What is it?

14 ANNE. It's hair shampoo. I took all the odds and ends of soap and mixed them with the last of my toilet water.

15 MRS. VAN DAAN. Oh, Anneke!

16 ANNE. I wanted to write a poem for all of them, but I didn't have time. [*offering a large box to* MR. VAN DAAN] Yours, Mr.

E

Van Daan, is *really* something . . . something you want
more than anything. [*As she waits for him to open it.*] Look!
Cigarettes!

2 MR. VAN DAAN. Cigarettes!

3 ANNE. Two of them! Pim found some old tobacco in the
pocket lining of his coat . . . and we made them . . . or
rather, Pim did.

4 MRS. VAN DAAN. Let me see . . . Well, look at that! Light it,
Putti! Light it.

MR. VAN DAAN *hesitates.*

5 ANNE. It's tobacco, really it is! There's a little fluff in it, but
not much.

Everyone watches intently as MR. VAN DAAN *cautiously lights it.
The cigarette flares up. Everyone laughs.*

6 PETER. It works!

7 MRS. VAN DAAN. Look at him.

8 MR. VAN DAAN [*spluttering*]. Thank you, Anne. Thank you.

ANNE *rushes back to her satchel for another present.*

9 ANNE [*handing her mother a piece of paper*]. For Mother, Hanukkah
greeting.

She pulls her mother to her feet.

10 MRS. FRANK [*She reads*]. 'Here's an I.O.U. that I promise to pay.
Ten hours of doing whatever you say. Signed, Anne
Frank.'

MRS. FRANK, *touched, takes* ANNE *in her arms, holding her close.*

11 DUSSEL [*to* ANNE]. Ten hours of doing what you're told?
Anything you're told?

12 ANNE. That's right.

13 DUSSEL. You wouldn't want to sell that, Mrs. Frank?

1 MRS. FRANK. Never! This is the most precious gift I've ever had!

She sits, showing her present to the others. ANNE *hurries back to the satchel and pulls out a scarf, the scarf that* MR. FRANK *found in the first scene.*

2 ANNE [*offering it to her father*]. For Pim.

3 MR. FRANK. Anneke . . . I wasn't supposed to have a present!

He takes it, unfolding it and showing it to the others.

4 ANNE. It's a muffler . . . to put round your neck . . . like an ascot, you know. I made it myself out of odds and ends . . . I knitted it in the dark each night, after I'd gone to bed. I'm afraid it looks better in the dark!

5 MR. FRANK [*putting it on*]. It's fine. It fits me perfectly. Thank you, Annele.

ANNE *hands* PETER *a ball of paper, with a string attached to it.*

6 ANNE. That's for Mouschi.

7 PETER [*rising to bow*]. On behalf of Mouschi, I thank you.

8 ANNE [*hesitant, handing him a gift*]. And . . . this is yours . . . from Mrs. Quack Quack. [*As he holds it gingerly in his hands.*] Well . . . open it . . . Aren't you going to open it?

9 PETER. I'm scared to. I know something's going to jump out and hit me.

10 ANNE. No. It's nothing like that, really.

11 MRS. VAN DAAN [*as he is opening it*]. What is it, Peter? Go on. Show it.

12 ANNE [*excitedly*]. It's a safety razor!

13 DUSSEL. A what?

14 ANNE. A razor!

15 MRS. VAN DAAN [*looking at it*]. You didn't make that out of odds and ends.

1   ANNE [*to* PETER]. Miep got it for me. It's not new. It's second-hand. But you really do need a razor now.

2   DUSSEL. For what?

3   ANNE. Look on his upper lip ... you can see the beginning of a moustache.

4   DUSSEL. He wants to get rid of that? Put a little milk on it and let the cat lick it off.

5   PETER [*starting for his room*]. Think you're funny, don't you.

6   DUSSEL. Look! He can't wait! He's going in to try it!

7   PETER. I'm going to give Mouschi his present!

    He goes into his room, slamming the door behind him.

8   MR. VAN DAAN [*disgustedly*]. Mouschi, Mouschi, Mouschi.

    In the distance we hear a dog persistently barking. ANNE *brings a gift to* DUSSEL.

9   ANNE. And last but never least, my room-mate, Mr. Dussel.

10 DUSSEL. For me? You have something for me?

    He opens the small box she gives him.

11 ANNE. I made them myself.

12 DUSSEL [*puzzled*]. Capsules! Two capsules!

13 ANNE. They're ear-plugs!

14 DUSSEL. Ear-plugs?

15 ANNE. To put in your ears so you won't hear me when I thrash around at night. I saw them advertised in a magazine. They're not real ones ... I made them out of cotton and candle wax. Try them ... See if they don't work ... see if you can hear me talk ...

16 DUSSEL [*putting them in his ears*]. Wait now until I get them in ... so.

17 ANNE. Are you ready?

1 DUSSEL. Huh?

2 ANNE. Are you ready?

3 DUSSEL. Good God! They've gone inside! I can't get them out! [*They laugh as* MR. DUSSEL *jumps about, trying to shake the plugs out of his ears. Finally he gets them out. Putting them away.*] Thank you, Anne! Thank you!

4 MR. VAN DAAN. A real Hanukkah!

5 MRS. VAN DAAN. Wasn't it cute of her?

6 MRS. FRANK. I don't know when she did it.   *together*

7 MARGOT. I love my present.

8 ANNE [*sitting at the table*]. And now let's have the song, Father ... please ... [*to* DUSSEL] Have you heard the Hanukkah song, Mr. Dussel? The song is the whole thing! [*She sings.*] 'Oh, Hanukkah! Oh Hanukkah! The sweet celebration ...'

9 MR. FRANK [*quieting her*]. I'm afraid, Anne, we shouldn't sing that song tonight. [*to* DUSSEL] It's a song of jubilation, of rejoicing. One is apt to become too enthusiastic.

10 ANNE. Oh, please, please. Let's sing the song. I promise not to shout!

11 MR. FRANK. Very well. But quietly now ... I'll keep an eye on you and when ...

   As ANNE *starts to sing, she is interrupted by* DUSSEL, *who is snorting and wheezing.*

12 DUSSEL [*pointing to* PETER]. You ... You! [PETER *is coming from his bedroom, ostentatiously holding a bulge in his coat as if he were holding his cat, and dangling* ANNE'S *present before it.*] How many times ... I told you ... Out! Out!

13 MR. VAN DAAN [*going to* PETER]. What's the matter with you? Haven't you any sense? Get that cat out of here.

14 PFTER [*innocently*]. Cat?

53

1 MR. VAN DAAN. You heard me. Get it out of here!

2 PETER. I have no cat.

   Delighted with his joke, he opens his coat and pulls out a bath towel. The group at the table laugh, enjoying the joke.

3 DUSSEL [*still wheezing*]. It doesn't need to be the cat . . . his clothes are enough . . . when he comes out of that room . . .

4 MR. VAN DAAN. Don't worry. You won't be bothered any more. We're getting rid of it.

5 DUSSEL. At last you listen to me.

   He goes off into his bedroom.

6 MR. VAN DAAN [*calling after him*]. I'm not doing it for you. That's all in your mind . . . all of it! [*He starts back to his place at the table.*] I'm doing it because I'm sick of seeing that cat eat all our food.

7 PETER. That's not true! I only give him bones . . . scraps . . .

8 MR. VAN DAAN. Don't tell me! He gets fatter every day! Damn cat looks better than any of us. Out he goes tonight!

9 PETER. No! No!

10 ANNE. Mr. Van Daan, you can't do that! That's Peter's cat. Peter loves that cat.

11 MRS. FRANK [*quietly*]. Anne.

12 PETER [*to* MR. VAN DAAN]. If he goes, I go.

13 MR. VAN DAAN. Go! Go!

14 MRS. VAN DAAN. You're not going and the cat's not going! Now please . . . this is Hanukkah . . . Hanukkah . . . this is the time to celebrate . . . What's the matter with all of you? Come on, Anne. Let's have the song.

15 ANNE [*singing*]. 'Oh, Hanukkah! Oh, Hanukkah! The sweet celebration.'

1   MR. FRANK [*rising*]. I think we should first blow out the candle
    . . . then we'll have something for tomorrow night.

2   MARGOT. But, Father, you're supposed to let it burn itself out.

3   MR. FRANK. I'm sure that God understands shortages. [*before
    blowing it out*] 'Praised be Thou, oh Lord our God, who
    hast sustained us and permitted us to celebrate this
    joyous festival.'

    *He is about to blow out the candle when suddenly there is a crash of
    something falling below. They all freeze in horror, motionless. For a
    few seconds there is complete silence. MR. FRANK slips off his shoes.
    The others noiselessly follow his example. MR. FRANK turns out a
    light near him. He motions to PETER to turn off the centre lamp.
    PETER tries to reach it, realizes he cannot and gets up on a chair.
    Just as he is touching the lamp he loses his balance. The chair goes
    out from under him. He falls. The iron lamp shade crashes to the
    floor. There is a sound of feet below, running down the stairs.*

4   MR. VAN DAAN [*under his breath*]. God Almighty! [*The only light
    left comes from the Hanukkah candle. DUSSEL comes from his room.
    MR. FRANK creeps over to the stair-well and stands listening. The
    dog is heard barking excitedly.*] Do you hear anything?

5   MR. FRANK [*in a whisper*]. No. I think they've gone.

6   MRS. VAN DAAN. It's the Green Police. They've found us.

7   MR. FRANK. If they had, they wouldn't have left. They'd be
    up here by now.

8   MRS. VAN DAAN. I know it's the Green Police. They've gone to
    get help. That's all. They'll be back!

9   MR. VAN DAAN. Or it may have been the Gestapo, looking for
    papers . . .

10 MR. FRANK [*interrupting*]. Or a thief, looking for money.

11 MRS. VAN DAAN. We've got to do something . . . Quick!
    Quick! Before they come back.

12 MR. VAN DAAN. There isn't anything to do. Just wait.

MR. FRANK *holds up his hand for them to be quiet. He is listening intently. There is complete silence as they all strain to hear any sound from below. Suddenly* ANNE *begins to sway. With a low cry she falls to the floor in a faint.* MRS. FRANK *goes to her quickly, sitting beside her on the floor and taking her in her arms.*

1 MRS. FRANK. Get some water, please! Get some water!

MARGOT *starts for the sink.*

2 MR. VAN DAAN [*grabbing* MARGOT]. No! No! No one's going to run water!

3 MR. FRANK. If they've found us, they've found us. Get the water. [MARGOT *starts again for the sink.* MR. FRANK, *getting a flashlight.*] I'm going down.

MARGOT *rushes to him, clinging to him.* ANNE *struggles to consciousness.*

4 MARGOT. No, Father, no! There may be someone there, waiting . . . It may be a trap!

5 MR. FRANK. This is Saturday. There is no way for us to know what has happened until Miep or Mr. Kraler comes on Monday morning. We cannot live with this uncertainty.

6 MARGOT. Don't go, Father!

7 MRS. FRANK. Hush, darling, hush. [MR. FRANK *slips quietly out, down the steps and out through the door below.*] Margot! Stay close to me.

MARGOT *goes to her mother.*

8 MR. VAN DAAN. Shush! Shush!

MRS. FRANK *whispers to* MARGOT *to get the water.* MARGOT *goes for it.*

9 MRS. VAN DAAN. Putti, where's our money? Get our money· I hear you can buy the Green Police off, so much a head· Go upstairs quick! Get the money!

10 MR. VAN DAAN. Keep still!

11 MRS. VAN DAAN [*kneeling before him, pleading*]. Do you want to be

Anne:

Good evening everyone.
Forgive me if I don't stay.
I have a friend waiting
for me in there. My
friend Tom. Tom Cat.
(*Page 20, speech 5*)

Anne:

I'm a terrible coward . . .
I think I've conquered my
fear . . . and then some-
thing happens and I run
to you like a baby. (*Page*
44, speech 12)

Mr. Kraler visits the loft.

Mrs. Van Dann: *It's been ages since I even saw a cake. Not since you brought one last year.* (Page 63, speech 6)

Anne: *Look at the sky now. Isn't it lovely?* (Page 95, speech 6)

dragged off to a concentration camp? Are you going to stand there and wait for them to come up and get you? Do something, I tell you!

2 MR. VAN DAAN [*pushing her aside*]. Will you keep still!

He goes over to the stair-well to listen. PETER *goes to his mother, helping her up on to the sofa. There is a second of silence, then* ANNE *can stand it no longer.*

3 ANNE. Someone go after Father! Make Father come back!

4 PETER [*starting for the door*]. I'll go.

5 MR. VAN DAAN. Haven't you done enough?

He pushes PETER *roughly away. In his anger against his father* PETER *grabs a chair as if to hit him with it, then puts it down, burying his face in his hands.* MRS. FRANK *begins to pray softly.*

6 ANNE. Please, please, Mr. Van Daan. Get Father.

7 MR. VAN DAAN. Quiet! Quiet!

ANNE *is shocked into silence.* MRS. FRANK *pulls her closer, holding her protectively in her arms.*

8 MRS. FRANK [*softly, praying*]. 'I lift up mine eyes unto the mountains, from whence cometh my help. My help cometh from the Lord who made heaven and earth. He will not suffer thy foot to be moved . . . He that keepeth thee will not slumber . . .'

She stops as she hears someone coming. They all watch the door tensely. MR. FRANK *comes quietly in.* ANNE *rushes to him, holding him tight.*

9 MR. FRANK. It was a thief. That noise must have scared him away.

10 MRS. VAN DAAN. Thank God.

11 MR. FRANK. He took the cash box. And the radio. He ran away in such a hurry that he didn't stop to shut the street door. It was swinging wide open. [*A breath of relief*

sweeps over them.] I think it would be good to have some light.

2   MARGOT. Are you sure it's all right?

3   MR. FRANK. The danger has passed. [MARGOT *goes to light the small lamp.*] Don't be so terrified, Anne. We're safe.

4   DUSSEL. Who says the danger has passed? Don't you realize we are in greater danger than ever?

5   MR. FRANK. Mr. Dussel, will you be still!

   MR. FRANK *takes* ANNE *back to the table, making her sit down with him, trying to calm her.*

6   DUSSEL [*pointing to* PETER]. Thanks to this clumsy fool, there's someone now who knows we're up here! Someone now knows we're up here, hiding!

7   MRS. VAN DAAN [*going to* DUSSEL]. Someone knows we're here, yes. But who is the someone? A thief! A thief! You think a thief is going to go to the Green Police and say ... I was robbing a place the other night and I heard a noise up over my head? You think a thief is going to do that?

8   DUSSEL. Yes. I think he will.

9   MRS. VAN DAAN [*hysterically*]. You're crazy!

   She stumbles back to her seat at the table. PETER *follows protectively, pushing* DUSSEL *aside.*

10   DUSSEL. I think some day he'll be caught and then he'll make a bargain with the Green Police ... if they'll let him off, he'll tell them where some Jews are hiding!

   He goes off into the bedroom. There is a second of appalled silence.

11   MR. VAN DAAN. He's right.

12   ANNE. Father, let's get out of here! We can't stay here now ... Let's go ...

13   MR. VAN DAAN. Go! Where?

1   MRS. FRANK [*sinking into her chair at the table*]. Yes. Where?

2   MR. FRANK [*rising, to them all*]. Have we lost faith? All courage?
A moment ago we thought that they'd come for us.
We were sure it was the end. But it wasn't the end.
We're alive, safe. [MR. VAN DAAN *goes to the table and sits.*
MR. FRANK *prays*] 'We thank Thee, oh Lord our God, that
in Thy infinite mercy Thou hast again seen fit to spare
us.' [*He blows out the candle, then turns to* ANNE.] Come on,
Anne. The song! Let's have the song! [*He starts to sing.*
ANNE *finally starts falteringly to sing, as* MR. FRANK *urges her on.
Her voice is hardly audible at first.*]

3   ANNE [*singing*].
    'Oh, Hanukkah! Oh, Hanukkah!
    The sweet . . . celebration . . .'

*As she goes on singing, the others gradually join in, their voices still
shaking with fear.* MRS. VAN DAAN *sobs as she sings.*

4   GROUP.
    'Around the feast . . . we . . . gather
    In complete . . . jubilation . . .
    Happiest of sea . . . sons
    Now is here.
    Many are the reasons for good cheer.'

DUSSEL *comes from the bedroom. He comes over to the table, standing
beside* MARGOT, *listening to them as they sing.*

    'Together
    We'll weather
    Whatever tomorrow may bring.'

As they sing on with growing courage, the lights start to dim.

    'So hear us rejoicing
    And merrily voicing
    The Hanukkah song that we sing.
    Hoy!'

The lights are out. The curtain starts slowly to fall.

'Hear us rejoicing
And merrily voicing
The Hanukkah song that we sing.'

They are still singing, as the curtain falls.

CURTAIN

Act 2

SCENE I

In the darkness we hear ANNE'S VOICE, *again reading from the diary.*

1 ANNE'S VOICE. Saturday, the first of January, nineteen forty-four. Another new year has begun and we find ourselves still in our hiding place. We have been here now for one year, five months and twenty-five days. It seems that our life is at a standstill . . .

The curtain rises on the scene. It is late afternoon. Everyone is bundled up against the cold. In the main room MRS. FRANK *is taking down the laundry which is hung across the back.* MR. FRANK *sits in the chair down left, reading.* MARGOT *is lying on the couch with a blanket over her and the many-coloured knitted scarf around her throat.* ANNE *is seated at the centre table, writing in her diary.* PETER, MR. *and* MRS. VAN DAAN *and* DUSSEL *are all in their own rooms, reading or lying down.*

As the lights dim on, ANNE'S VOICE *continues, without a break.*

We are all a little thinner. The Van Daans' 'discussions' are as violent as ever. Mother still does not understand me. But then I don't understand her either. There is one great change, however. A change in myself. I read somewhere that girls of my age don't feel quite certain of themselves. That they become quiet within and begin to think of the miracle that is taking place in their bodies. I think that what is happening to me is so wonderful . . . not only what can be seen, but what is taking place inside. Each time it has happened I have a feeling that I have a sweet secret. [*We hear the chimes and then a hymn being played on the carillon outside.*] And in spite of any pain, I long for the time when I shall feel that secret within me again.

The buzzer of the door below suddenly sounds. Everyone is startled. MR. FRANK *tiptoes cautiously to the top of the steps and listens. Again the buzzer sounds, in* MIEP'S *V-for-Victory signal.*

1   MR. FRANK. It's Miep!

> *He goes quickly down the steps to unbolt the door.* MRS. FRANK *calls upstairs to the* VAN DAANS *and then to* PETER.

2   MRS. FRANK. Wake up, everyone! Miep is here! [ANNE *quickly puts her diary away.* MARGOT *sits up, pulling the blanket around her shoulders.* MR. DUSSEL *sits on the edge of his bed, listening, disgruntled.* MIEP *comes up the steps, followed by* MR. KRALER. *They bring flowers, books, newspapers, etc.* ANNE *rushes to* MIEP, *throwing her arms affectionately around her.*] Miep . . . and Mr. Kraler . . . What a delightful surprise!

3   MR. KRALER. We came to bring you New Year's greetings.

4   MRS. FRANK. You shouldn't . . . you should have at least one day to yourselves.

> *She goes quickly to the stove and brings down teacups and tea for all of them.*

5   ANNE. Don't say that, it's so wonderful to see them! [*Sniffing at* MIEP's *coat.*] I can smell the wind and the cold on your clothes.

6   MIEP [*giving her the flowers*]. There you are. [*Then to* MARGOT, *feeling her forehead.*] How are you, Margot? . . . Feeling any better?

7   MARGOT. I'm all right.

8   ANNE. We filled her full of every kind of pill so she won't cough and make a noise.

> *She runs into her room to put the flowers in water.* MR. *and* MRS. VAN DAAN *come from upstairs. Outside there is the sound of a band playing.*

9   MRS. VAN DAAN. Well, hello, Miep. Mr. Kraler.

10   MR. KRALER [*giving a bouquet of flowers to* MRS. VAN DAAN]. With my hope for peace in the New Year.

11   PETER [*anxiously*]. Miep, have you seen Mouschi? Have you seen him anywhere around?

1 MIEP. I'm sorry, Peter. I asked everyone in the neighbour-hood had they seen a grey cat. But they said no.

    MRS. FRANK *gives* MIEP *a cup of tea.* MR. FRANK *comes up the steps, carrying a small cake on a plate.*

2 MR. FRANK. Look what Miep's brought for us!

3 MRS. FRANK [*taking it*]. A cake!

4 MR. VAN DAAN. A cake! [*He pinches* MIEP'S *cheeks gaily and hurries up to the cupboard.*] I'll get some plates.

    DUSSEL, *in his room, hastily puts a coat on and starts out to join the others.*

5 MRS. FRANK. Thank you, Miepia. You shouldn't have done it. You must have used all of your sugar ration for weeks. [*giving it to* MRS. VAN DAAN] It's beautiful, isn't it?

6 MRS. VAN DAAN. It's been ages since I even saw a cake. Not since you brought us one last year. [*without looking at the cake, to* MIEP] Remember? Don't you remember, you gave us one on New Year's Day? Just this time last year? I'll never forget it because you had 'Peace in nineteen forty-three' on it. [*She looks at the cake and reads*]. 'Peace in nineteen forty-four!'

7 MIEP. Well, it has to come sometime, you know. [*As* DUSSEL *comes from his room.*] Hello, Mr. Dussel.

8 MR. KRALER. How are you?

9 MR. VAN DAAN [*bringing plates and a knife*]. Here's the knife, *liefje.* Now, how many of us are there?

10 MIEP. None for me, thank you.

11 MR. FRANK. Oh, please. You must.

12 MIEP. I couldn't.

13 MR. VAN DAAN. Good! That leaves one . . . two . . . three . . . seven of us.

14 DUSSEL. Eight! Eight! It's the same number as it always is!

1   MR. VAN DAAN. I left Margot out. I take it for granted Margot won't eat any.

2   ANNE. Why wouldn't she!

3   MRS. FRANK. I think it won't harm her.

4   MR. VAN DAAN. All right! All right! I just didn't want her to start coughing again, that's all.

5   DUSSEL. And please, Mrs. Frank should cut the cake.

6   MR. VAN DAAN. What's the difference?

7   MRS. VAN DAAN. It's not Mrs. Frank's cake, is it Miep? It's for all of us.

together

8   DUSSEL. Mrs. Frank divides things better.

9   MRS. VAN DAAN [*going to* DUSSEL]. What are you trying to say?

10 MR. VAN DAAN. Oh, come on! Stop wasting time!

together

11 MRS. VAN DAAN [*to* DUSSEL]. Don't I always give everybody exactly the same? Don't I?

12 MR. VAN DAAN. Forget it, Kerli.

13 MRS. VAN DAAN. No. I want an answer! Don't I?

14 DUSSEL. Yes. Yes. Everybody gets exactly the same... except Mr. Van Daan always gets a little bit more.

VAN DAAN *advances on* DUSSEL, *the knife still in his hand.*

15 MR. VAN DAAN. That's a lie!

DUSSEL *retreats before the onslaught of the* VAN DAANS.

16 MR. FRANK. Please, please! [*then to* MIEP] You see what a little sugar cake does to us? It goes right to our heads!

17 MR. VAN DAAN [*handing* MRS. FRANK *the knife*]. Here you are, Mrs. Frank.

18 MRS. FRANK. Thank you. [*Then to* MIEP *as she goes to the table to cut the cake.*] Are you sure you won't have some?

1 MIEP [*drinking her tea*]. No, really, I have to go in a minute.

The sound of the band fades out in the distance.

2 PETER [*to* MIEP]. Maybe Mouschi went back to our house . . . they say that cats . . . Do you ever get over there . . . ? I mean . . . do you suppose you could . . . ?

3 MIEP. I'll try, Peter. The first minute I get I'll try. But I'm afraid, with him gone a week . . .

4 DUSSEL. Make up your mind, already someone has had a nice big dinner from that cat!

PETER *is furious, inarticulate. He starts towards* DUSSEL *as if to hit him.* MR. FRANK *stops him.* MRS. FRANK *speaks quickly to ease the situation.*

5 MRS. FRANK [*to* MIEP]. This is delicious, Miep!

6 MRS. VAN DAAN [*eating hers*]. Delicious!

7 MR. VAN DAAN [*finishing it in one gulp*]. Dirk's in luck to get a girl who can bake like this!

8 MIEP [*putting down her empty teacup*]. I have to run. Dirk's taking me to a party tonight.

9 ANNE. How heavenly! Remember now what everyone is wearing, and what you have to eat and everything, so you can tell us tomorrow.

10 MIEP. I'll give you a full report! Good-bye, everyone!

11 MR. VAN DAAN [*to* MIEP]. Just a minute. There's something I'd like you to do for me.

He hurries off up the stairs to his room.

12 MRS. VAN DAAN [*sharply*]. Putti, where are you going? [*She rushes up the stairs after him, calling hysterically.*] What do you want? Putti, what are you going to do?

13 MIEP [*to* PETER]. What's wrong?

14 PETER [*His sympathy is with his mother*]. Father says he's going to sell her fur coat. She's crazy about that old fur coat.

65

F

1 DUSSEL. Is it possible? Is it possible that anyone is so silly as to worry about a fur coat in times like this?

2 PETER. It's none of your darn business ... and if you say one more thing ... I'll, I'll take you and I'll ... I mean it ... I'll ...

There is a piercing scream from MRS. VAN DAAN *above. She grabs at the fur coat as* MR. VAN DAAN *is starting downstairs with it.*

3 MRS. VAN DAAN. No! No! No! Don't you dare take that! You hear? It's mine! [*Downstairs* PETER *turns away, embarrassed, miserable.*] My father gave me that! You didn't give it to me. You have no right. Let go of it ... you hear?

MR. VAN DAAN *pulls the coat from her hands and hurries downstairs.* MRS. VAN DAAN *sinks to the floor, sobbing. As* MR. VAN DAAN *comes into the main room the others look away, embarrassed for him.*

4 MR. VAN DAAN [*to* MR. KRALER]. Just a little—discussion over the advisability of selling this coat. As I have often reminded Mrs. Van Daan, it's very selfish of her to keep it when people outside are in such desperate need of clothing ... [*He gives the coat to* MIEP.] So if you will please to sell it for us? It should fetch a good price. And by the way, will you get me cigarettes. I don't care what kind they are ... get all you can.

5 MIEP. It's terribly difficult to get them, Mr. Van Daan. But I'll try. Good-bye.

She goes. MR. FRANK *follows her down the steps to bolt the door after her.* MRS. FRANK *gives* MR. KRALER *a cup of tea.*

6 MRS. FRANK. Are you sure you won't have some cake, Mr. Kraler?

7 MR. KRALER. I'd better not.

8 MR. VAN DAAN. You're still feeling badly? What does your doctor say?

9 MR. KRALER. I haven't been to him.

10 MRS. FRANK. Now, Mr. Kraler! ...

1 MR. KRALER [*sitting at the table*]. Oh, I tried. But you can't get near a doctor these days . . . they're so busy. After weeks I finally managed to get one on the telephone. I told him I'd like an appointment . . . I wasn't feeling very well. You know what he answers . . . over the telephone . . . Stick out your tongue! [*They laugh. He turns to* MR. FRANK *as* MR. FRANK *comes back.*] I have some contracts here . . . I wonder if you'd look over them with me . . .

2 MR. FRANK [*putting out his hand*]. Of course.

3 MR. KRALER [*He rises*]. If we could go downstairs . . . [MR. FRANK *starts ahead,* MR. KRALER *speaks to the others.*] Will you forgive us? I won't keep him but a minute.

He starts to follow MR. FRANK *down the steps.*

4 MARGOT [*with sudden foreboding*]. What's happened? Something's happened! Hasn't it, Mr. Kraler?

MR. KRALER *stops and comes back, trying to reassure* MARGOT *with a pretence of casualness.*

5 MR. KRALER. No, really. I want your father's advice . . .

6 MARGOT. Something's gone wrong! I know it!

7 MR. FRANK [*coming back, to* MR. KRALER]. If it's something that concerns us here, it's better that we all hear it.

8 MR. KRALER [*turning to him, quietly*]. But . . . the children . . . ?

9 MR. FRANK. What they'd imagine would be worse than any reality.

As MR. KRALER *speaks, they all listen with intense apprehension.* MRS. VAN DAAN *comes down the stairs and sits on the bottom step.*

10 MR. KRALER. It's a man in the store-room . . . I don't know whether or not you remember him . . . Carl, about fifty, heavy-set, near-sighted . . . He came with us just before you left.

11 MR. FRANK. He was from Utrecht?

12 MR. KRALER. That's the man. A couple of weeks ago, when I

was in the store-room, he closed the door and asked me . . . how's Mr. Frank? What do you hear from Mr. Frank? I told him I only knew there was a rumour that you were in Switzerland. He said he'd heard that rumour too, but he thought I might know something more. I didn't pay any attention to it . . . but then a thing happened yesterday . . . He'd brought some invoices to the office for me to sign. As I was going through them, I looked up. He was standing staring at the bookcase . . . your bookcase. He said he thought he remembered a door there . . . Wasn't there a door there that used to go up to the loft? Then he told me he wanted more money. Twenty guilders more a week.

2   MR. VAN DAAN. Blackmail!

3   MR. FRANK. Twenty guilders? Very modest blackmail.

4   MR. VAN DAAN. That's just the beginning.

5   DUSSEL [*coming to* MR. FRANK]. You know what I think? He was the thief who was down there that night. That's how he knows we're here.

6   MR. FRANK [*to* MR. KRALER]. How was it left? What did you tell him?

7   MR. KRALER. I said I had to think about it. What shall I do? Pay him the money? . . . Take a chance on firing him . . . or what? I don't know.

8   DUSSEL [*frantic*]. For God's sake don't fire him! Pay him what he asks . . . keep him here where you can have your eye on him.

9   MR. FRANK. Is it so much that he's asking? What are they paying nowadays?

10   MR. KRALER. He could get it in a war plant. But this isn't a war plant. Mind you, I don't know if he really knows . . . or if he doesn't know.

11   MR. FRANK. Offer him half. Then we'll soon find out if it's blackmail or not.

68

1   DUSSEL. And if it is? We've got to pay it, haven't we? Anything he asks we've got to pay!

2   MR. FRANK. Let's decide that when the time comes.

3   MR. KRALER. This may be all my imagination. You get to a point, these days, where you suspect everyone and everything. Again and again . . . on some simple look or word, I've found myself . . .

The telephone rings in the office below.

4   MRS. VAN DAAN [*hurrying to* MR. KRALER]. There's the telephone! What does that mean, the telephone ringing on a holiday?

5   MR. KRALER. That's my wife. I told her I had to go over some papers in my office . . . to call me there when she got out of church. [*He starts out.*] I'll offer him half then. Goodbye . . . we'll hope for the best!

The group call their good-byes half-heartedly. MR. FRANK *follows* MR. KRALER, *to bolt the door below. During the following scene,* MR. FRANK *comes back up and stands listening, disturbed.*

6   DUSSEL [*to* MR. VAN DAAN]. You can thank your son for this . . . smashing the light! I tell you, it's just a question of time now.

He goes to the window at the back and stands looking out.

7   MARGOT. Sometimes I wish the end would come . . . whatever it is.

8   MRS. FRANK [*shocked*]. Margot!

ANNE *goes to* MARGOT, *sitting beside her on the couch with her arms around her.*

9   MARGOT. Then at least we'd know where we were.

10 MRS. FRANK. You should be ashamed of yourself! Talking that way! Think how lucky we are! Think of the thousands dying in the war, every day. Think of the people in concentration camps.

1   ANNE [*interrupting*]. What's the good of that? What's the good
    of thinking of misery when you're already miserable?
    That's stupid!

2   MRS. FRANK. Anne!

    As ANNE *goes on raging at her mother,* MRS. FRANK *tries to break
    in, in an effort to quiet her.*

3   ANNE. We're young, Margot and Peter and I! You grown-
    ups have had your chance! But look at us . . . If we
    begin thinking of all the horror in the world, we're lost!
    We're trying to hold on to some kind of ideals . . . when
    everything . . . ideals, hopes . . . everything, are being
    destroyed! It isn't our fault that the world is in such a
    mess! We weren't around when all this started! So don't
    try to take it out on us!

    *She rushes off to her room, slamming the door after her. She picks up a
    brush from the chest and hurls it to the floor. Then she sits on the couch,
    trying to control her anger.*

4   MR. VAN DAAN. She talks as if we started the war! Did we
    start the war?

    He spots ANNE's *cake. As he starts to take it,* PETER *anticipates him.*

5   PETER. She left her cake. [*He starts for* ANNE's *room with the cake.
    There is silence in the main room.* MRS. VAN DAAN *goes up to her
    room, followed by* VAN DAAN. DUSSEL *stays looking out the window.*
    MR. FRANK *brings* MRS. FRANK *her cake. She eats it slowly,
    without relish.* MR. FRANK *takes his cake to* MARGOT *and sits quietly
    on the couch beside her.* PETER *stands in the doorway of* ANNE's
    *darkened room, looking at her, then makes a little movement to let
    her know he is there.* ANNE *sits up, quickly, trying to hide the signs
    of her tears.* PETER *holds out the cake to her.*] You left this.

6   ANNE [*dully*]. Thanks.

    PETER *starts to go out, then comes back.*

7   PETER. I thought you were fine just now. You know just
    how to talk to them. You know just how to say it. I'm
    no good . . . I never can think . . . especially when I'm

70

mad . . . That Dussel . . . when he said that about Mouschi . . . someone eating him . . . all I could think is . . . I wanted to hit him. I wanted to give him such a . . . a . . . that he'd . . . That's what I used to do when there was an argument at school . . . That's the way I . . . but here . . . And an old man like that . . . it wouldn't be so good.

2   ANNE. You're making a big mistake about me. I do it all wrong. I say too much. I go too far. I hurt people's feelings . . .

DUSSEL leaves the window, going to his room.

3   PETER. I think you're just fine . . . What I want to say . . . if it wasn't for you around here, I don't know. What I mean . . .

PETER is interrupted by DUSSEL's turning on the light. DUSSEL stands in the doorway, startled to see PETER. PETER advances towards him forbiddingly. DUSSEL backs out of the room. PETER closes the door on him.

4   ANNE. Do you mean it, Peter? Do you really mean it?

5   PETER. I said it, didn't I?

6   ANNE. Thank you, Peter!

In the main room MR. and MRS. FRANK collect the dishes and take them to the sink, washing them. MARGOT lies down again on the couch. DUSSEL, lost, wanders into PETER's room and takes up a book, starting to read.

7   PETER [looking at the photographs on the wall]. You've got quite a collection.

8   ANNE. Wouldn't you like some in your room? I could give you some. Heaven knows you spend enough time in there . . . doing heaven knows what . . .

9   PETER. It's easier. A fight starts, or an argument . . . I duck in there.

10   ANNE. You're lucky, having a room to go to. His lordship is

always here . . . I hardly ever get a minute alone. When they start in on me, I can't duck away. I have to stand there and take it.

2 PETER. You gave some of it back just now.

3 ANNE. I get so mad. They've formed their opinions . . . about everything . . . but we . . . we're still trying to find out . . . We have problems here that no other people our age have ever had. And just as you think you've solved them, something comes along and bang! You have to start all over again.

4 PETER. At least you've got someone you can talk to.

5 ANNE. Not really. Mother . . . I never discuss anything serious with her. She doesn't understand. Father's all right. We can talk about everything . . . everything but one thing. Mother. He simply won't talk about her. I don't think you can be really intimate with anyone if he holds something back, do you?

6 PETER. I think your father's fine.

7 ANNE. Oh, he is, Peter! He is! He's the only one who's ever given me the feeling that I have any sense. But anyway, nothing can take the place of school and play and friends of your own age . . . or near your age . . . can it?

8 PETER. I suppose you miss your friends and all.

9 ANNE. It isn't just . . . [*She breaks off, staring up at him for a second.*] Isn't it funny, you and I? Here we've been seeing each other every minute for almost a year and a half, and this is the first time we've ever really talked. It helps a lot to have someone to talk to, don't you think? It helps you to let off steam.

10 PETER [*going to the door*]. Well, any time you want to let off steam, you can come into my room.

11 ANNE [*following him*]. I can get up an awful lot of steam. You'll have to be careful how you say that.

1　PETER. It's all right with me.

2　ANNE. Do you mean it?

3　PETER. I said it, didn't I?

> *He goes out.* ANNE *stands in her doorway looking after him. As* PETER *goes to his door he stands for a minute looking back at her. Then he goes into his room.* DUSSEL *rises as he comes in, and quickly passes him, going out. He starts across for his room.* ANNE *sees him coming, and pulls her door shut.* DUSSEL *turns back toward* PETER'S *room.* PETER *pulls his door shut.* DUSSEL *stands there, bewildered, forlorn.*
> *The scene slowly dims out. The curtain falls on the scene.* ANNE'S VOICE *comes over in the darkness . . . faintly at first, and then with growing strength.*

4　ANNE'S VOICE. We've had bad news. The people from whom Miep got our ration books have been arrested. So we have had to cut down on our food. Our stomachs are so empty that they rumble and make strange noises, all in different keys. Mr. Van Daan's is deep and low, like a bass fiddle. Mine is high, whistling like a flute. As we all sit around waiting for supper, it's like an orchestra tuning up. It only needs Toscanini to raise his baton and we'd be off in the Ride of the Valkyries. Monday, the sixth of March, nineteen forty-four. Mr. Kraler is in the hospital. It seems he has ulcers. Pim says we are his ulcers. Miep has to run the business and us too. The Americans have landed on the southern tip of Italy. Father looks for a quick finish to the war. Mr. Dussel is waiting every day for the warehouse man to demand more money. Have I been skipping too much from one subject to another? I can't help it. I feel that spring is coming. I feel it in my whole body and soul. I feel utterly confused. I am longing . . . so longing . . . for everything . . . for friends . . . for someone to talk to . . . someone who understands . . . someone young, who feels as I do . . .

> *As these last lines are being said, the curtain rises on the scene. The lights dim on.* ANNE'S VOICE *fades out.*

73

SCENE 2

It is evening, after supper. From outside we hear the sound of children playing. The 'grown-ups', with the exception of MR. VAN DAAN, *are all in the main room.* MRS. FRANK *is doing some mending.* MRS. VAN DAAN *is reading a fashion magazine.* MR. FRANK *is going over business accounts.* DUSSEL, *in his dentist's jacket, is pacing up and down, impatient to get into his bedroom.* MR. VAN DAAN *is upstairs working on a piece of embroidery in an embroidery frame.*
In his room PETER *is sitting before the mirror, smoothing his hair. As the scene goes on, he puts on his tie, brushes his coat and puts it on, preparing himself meticulously for a visit from* ANNE. *On his wall are now hung some of* ANNE'S *film stars.*
In her room ANNE *too is getting dressed. She stands before the mirror in her slip, trying various ways of dressing her hair.* MARGOT *is seated on the sofa, hemming a skirt for* ANNE *to wear.*
In the main room DUSSEL *can stand it no longer. He comes over, rapping sharply on the door of his and* ANNE'S *bedroom.*

1   ANNE [*calling to him*]. No, no, Mr. Dussel! I am not dressed yet. [DUSSEL *walks away, furious, sitting down and burying his head in his hands.* ANNE *turns to* MARGOT.] How is that? How does that look?

2   MARGOT [*glancing at her briefly*]. Fine.

3   ANNE. You didn't even look.

4   MARGOT. Of course I did. It's fine.

5   ANNE. Margot, tell me, am I terribly ugly?

6   MARGOT. Oh, stop fishing.

7   ANNE. No. No. Tell me.

8   MARGOT. Of course, you're not. You've got nice eyes . . . and a lot of animation, and . . .

9   ANNE. A little vague, aren't you?

She reaches over and takes a brassière out of MARGOT'S *sewing basket. She holds it up to herself, studying the effect in the mirror. Outside,*

MRS. FRANK, *feeling sorry for* DUSSEL, *comes over, knocking at the girl's door.*

1   MRS. FRANK [*outside*]. May I come in?

2   MARGOT. Come in, Mother.

3   MRS. FRANK [*shutting the door behind her*]. Mr. Dussel's impatient to get in here.

4   ANNE [*still with the brassière*]. Heaven's, he takes the room for himself the entire day.

5   MRS. FRANK [*gently*]. Anne, dear, you're not going in again tonight to see Peter?

6   ANNE [*dignified*]. That is my intention.

7   MRS. FRANK. But you've already spent a great deal of time in there today.

8   ANNE. I was in there exactly twice. Once to get the dictionary, and then three-quarters of an hour before supper.

9   MRS. FRANK. Aren't you afraid you're disturbing him?

10   ANNE. Mother, I have some intuition.

11   MRS. FRANK. Then may I ask you this much, Anne. Please don't shut the door when you go in.

12   ANNE. You sound like Mrs. Van Daan!

She throws the brassière in MARGOT'S *sewing basket and picks up her blouse, putting it on.*

13   MRS. FRANK. No. No. I don't mean to suggest anything wrong. I only wish that you wouldn't expose yourself to criticism . . . that you wouldn't give Mrs. Van Daan the opportunity to be unpleasant.

14   ANNE. Mrs. Van Daan doesn't need an opportunity to be unpleasant!

15   MRS. FRANK. Everyone's on edge, worried about Mr. Kraler. This is one more thing . . .

1 ANNE. I'm sorry, Mother. I'm going to Peter's room. I'm not going to let Petronella Van Daan spoil our friendship.

MRS. FRANK hesitates for a second, then goes out, closing the door after her. She gets a pack of playing cards and sits at the centre table, playing solitaire. In ANNE'S room MARGOT hands the finished skirt to ANNE. As ANNE is putting it on, MARGOT takes off her high-heeled shoes and stuffs paper in the toes so that ANNE can wear them.

2 MARGOT [*to* ANNE]. Why don't you two talk in the main room? It'd save a lot of trouble. It's hard on Mother, having to listen to those remarks from Mrs. Van Daan and not say a word.

3 ANNE. Why doesn't she say a word? I think it's ridiculous to take it and take it.

4 MARGOT. You don't understand Mother at all, do you? She can't talk back. She's not like you. It's just not in her nature to fight back.

5 ANNE. Anyway . . . the only one I worry about is you. I feel awfully guilty about you.

She sits on the stool near MARGOT, *putting on* MARGOT'S *high-heeled shoes.*

6 MARGOT. What about?

7 ANNE. I mean, every time I go into Peter's room, I have a feeling I may be hurting you. [MARGOT *shakes her head.*] I know if it were me, I'd be wild. I'd be desperately jealous, if it were me.

8 MARGOT. Well, I'm not.

9 ANNE. You don't feel badly? Really? Truly? You're not jealous?

10 MARGOT. Of course I'm jealous . . . jealous that you've got something to get up in the morning for . . . But jealous of you and Peter? No.

ANNE goes back to the mirror.

1　ANNE. Maybe there's nothing to be jealous of. Maybe he doesn't really like me. Maybe I'm just taking the place of his cat . . . [*She picks up a pair of short white gloves, putting them on.*] Wouldn't you like to come in with us?

2　MARGOT. I have a book.

The sound of the children playing outside fades out. In the main room DUSSEL *can stand it no longer. He jumps up, going to the bedroom door and knocking sharply.*

3　DUSSEL. Will you please let me in my room!

4　ANNE. Just a minute, dear, dear Mr. Dussel. [*She picks up her mother's pink stole and adjusts it elegantly over her shoulders, then gives a last look in the mirror.*] Well, here I go . . . to run the gauntlet.

She starts out, followed by MARGOT.

5　DUSSEL [*as she appears—sarcastic*]. Thank you so much.

DUSSEL goes into his room. ANNE goes towards PETER'S room, passing MRS. VAN DAAN and her parents at the centre table.

6　MRS. VAN DAAN. My God, look at her! [ANNE *pays no attention. She knocks at* PETER'S *door.*] I don't know what good it is to have a son. I never see him. He wouldn't care if I killed myself. [PETER *opens the door and stands aside for* ANNE *to come in.*] Just a minute, Anne. [*She goes to them at the door.*] I'd like to say a few words to my son. Do you mind? [PETER *and* ANNE *stand waiting.*] Peter, I don't want you staying up till all hours tonight. You've got to have your sleep. You're a growing boy. You hear?

7　MRS. FRANK. Anne won't stay late. She's going to bed promptly at nine. Aren't you, Anne?

8　ANNE. Yes, Mother . . . [*to* MRS. VAN DAAN] May we go now?

9　MRS. VAN DAAN. Are you asking me? I didn't know I had anything to say about it.

1 MRS. FRANK. Listen for the chimes, Anne dear.

The two young people go off into PETER'S *room, shutting the door after them.*

2 MRS. VAN DAAN [*to* MRS. FRANK]. In my day it was the boys who called on the girls. Not the girls on the boys.

3 MRS. FRANK. You know how young people like to feel that they have secrets. Peter's room is the only place where they can talk.

4 MRS. VAN DAAN. Talk! That's not what they called it when I was young.

MRS. VAN DAAN goes off to the bathroom. MARGOT *settles down to read her book.* MR. FRANK *puts his papers away and brings a chess game to the centre table. He and* MRS. FRANK *start to play. In* PETER'S *room,* ANNE *speaks to* PETER, *indignant, humiliated.*

5 ANNE. Aren't they awful? Aren't they impossible? Treating us as if we were still in the nursery.

She sits on the cot. PETER *gets a bottle of lemonade and two glasses.*

6 PETER. Don't let it bother you. It doesn't bother me.

7 ANNE. I suppose you can't really blame them . . . they think back to what *they* were like at our age. They don't realize how much more advanced we are . . . When you think what wonderful discussions we've had! . . . Oh, I forgot. I was going to bring you some more pictures.

8 PETER. Oh, these are fine, thanks.

9 ANNE. Don't you want some more? Miep just brought me some new ones.

10 PETER. Maybe later.

He gives her a glass of lemonade and, taking some for himself, sits down facing her.

11 ANNE [*looking up at one of the photographs*]. I remember when I got that . . . I won it. I bet Jopie that I could eat five ice-cream cones. We'd all been playing ping-pong . . . We used to

have heavenly times . . . we'd finish up with ice cream at the Delphi, or the Oasis, where Jews were allowed . . . there'd always be a lot of boys . . . we'd laugh and joke . . . I'd like to go back to it for a few days or a week. But after that I know I'd be bored to death. I think more seriously about life now. I want to be a journalist . . . or something. I love to write. What do you want to do?

2   PETER. I thought I might go off some place . . . work on a farm or something . . . some job that doesn't take much brains.

3   ANNE. You shouldn't talk that way. You've got the most awful inferiority complex.

4   PETER. I know I'm not clever.

5   ANNE. That isn't true. You're much better than I am in dozens of things . . . arithmetic and algebra and . . . well, you're a million times better than I am in algebra. [*with sudden directness*] You like Margot, don't you? Right from the start you liked her, liked her much better than me.

6   PETER [*uncomfortably*]. Oh, I don't know.

In the main room MRS. VAN DAAN *comes from the bathroom and goes over to the sink, polishing a coffee pot.*

7   ANNE. It's all right. Everyone feels that way. Margot's so good. She's sweet and bright and beautiful and I'm not.

8   PETER. I wouldn't say that.

9   ANNE. Oh, no, I'm not. I know that. I know quite well that I'm not a beauty. I never have been and never shall be.

10   PETER. I don't agree at all. I think you're pretty.

11   ANNE. That's not true!

12   PETER. And another thing. You've changed . . . from at first, I mean.

13   ANNE. I have?

1 PETER. I used to think you were awfully noisy.

2 ANNE. And what do you think now, Peter? How have I changed?

3 PETER. Well . . . er . . . you're . . . quieter.

   In his room DUSSEL *takes his pyjamas and toilet articles and goes into the bathroom to change.*

4 ANNE. I'm glad you don't just hate me.

5 PETER. I never said that.

6 ANNE. I bet when you get out of here you'll never think of me again.

7 PETER. That's crazy.

8 ANNE. When you get back with all of your friends, you're going to say . . . now what did I ever see in that Mrs. Quack Quack.

9 PETER. I haven't got any friends.

10 ANNE. Oh, Peter, of course you have. Everyone has friends.

11 PETER. Not me. I don't want any. I get along all right without them.

12 ANNE. Does that mean you can get along without me? I think of myself as your friend.

13 PETER. No. If they were all like you, it'd be different.

   He takes the glasses and the bottle and puts them away. There is a second's silence and then ANNE *speaks, hesitantly, shyly.*

14 ANNE. Peter, did you ever kiss a girl?

15 PETER. Yes. Once.

16 ANNE [*to cover her feelings*]. That picture's crooked. [PETER *goes over, straightening the photograph.*] Was she pretty?

17 PETER. Huh?

18 ANNE. The girl that you kissed.

1 PETER. I don't know. I was blindfolded. [*He comes back and sits down again.*] It was at a party. One of those kissing games.

2 ANNE [*relieved*]. Oh. I don't suppose that really counts, does it?

3 PETER. It didn't with me.

4 ANNE. I've been kissed twice. Once a man I'd never seen before kissed me on the cheek when he picked me up off the ice and I was crying. And the other was Mr. Koophuis, a friend of Father's who kissed my hand. You wouldn't say those counted, would you?

5 PETER. I wouldn't say so.

6 ANNE. I know almost for certain that Margot would never kiss anyone unless she was engaged to them. And I'm sure too that Mother never touched a man before Pim. But I don't know ... things are so different now ... What do you think? Do you think a girl shouldn't kiss anyone except if she's engaged or something? It's so hard to try to think what to do, when here we are with the whole world falling around our ears and you think ... well ... you don't know what's going to happen tomorrow and ... What do you think?

7 PETER. I suppose it'd depend on the girl. Some girls, anything they do's wrong. But others ... well ... it wouldn't necessarily be wrong with them. [*The carillon starts to strike nine o'clock.*] I've always thought that when two people ...

8 ANNE. Nine o'clock. I have to go.

9 PETER. That's right.

10 ANNE [*without moving*]. Good night.

There is a second's pause, then PETER *gets up and moves towards the door.*

11 PETER. You won't let them stop you coming?

12 ANNE. No. [*She rises and starts for the door.*] Sometime I might

81

bring my diary. There are so many things in it that I want to talk over with you. There's a lot about you.

2 PETER. What kind of thing?

3 ANNE. I wouldn't want you to see some of it. I thought you were a nothing, just the way you thought about me.

4 PETER. Did you change your mind, the way I changed my mind about you?

5 ANNE. Well . . . You'll see . . .

For a second ANNE *stands looking up at* PETER, *longing for him to kiss her. As he makes no move she turns away. Then suddenly* PETER *grabs her awkwardly in his arms, kissing her on the cheek.* ANNE *walks out dazed. She stands for a minute, her back to the people in the main room. As she regains her poise she goes to her mother and father and* MARGOT, *silently kissing them. They murmur their good nights to her. As she is about to open her bedroom door, she catches sight of* MRS. VAN DAAN. *She goes quickly to her, taking her face in her hands and kissing her first on one cheek and then on the other. Then she hurries off into her room.* MRS. VAN DAAN *looks after her, and then looks over at* PETER'S *room. Her suspicions are confirmed.*

6 MRS. VAN DAAN [*She knows*]. Ah hah!

The lights dim out. The curtain falls on the scene. In the darkness ANNE'S VOICE *comes faintly at first and then with growing strength.*

7 ANNE'S VOICE. By this time we all know each other so well that if anyone starts to tell a story, the rest can finish it for him. We're having to cut down still further on our meals. What makes it worse, the rats have been at work again. They've carried off some of our precious food. Even Mr. Dussel wishes now that Mouschi was here. Thursday, the twentieth of April, nineteen forty-four. Invasion fever is mounting every day. Miep tells us that people outside talk of nothing else. For myself, life has become much more pleasant. I often go to Peter's room after supper. Oh, don't think I'm in love, because I'm not. But it does make life more bearable to have someone with whom you can exchange views. No more

tonight. P.S. . . . I must be honest. I must confess that I actually live for the next meeting. Is there anything lovelier than to sit under the skylight and feel the sun on your cheeks and have a darling boy in your arms? I admit now that I'm glad the Van Daans had a son and not a daughter. I've outgrown another dress. That's the third. I'm having to wear Margot's clothes after all. I'm working hard on my French and am now reading *La Belle Nivernaise.*

As she is saying the last lines—the curtain rises on the scene. The lights dim on, as ANNE'S VOICE *fades out.*

SCENE 3

It is night, a few weeks later. Everyone is in bed. There is complete quiet. In the VAN DAANS' *room a match flares up for a moment and then is quickly put out.* MR. VAN DAAN, *in bare feet, dressed in underwear and trousers, is dimly seen coming stealthily down the stairs and into the main room, where* MR. *and* MRS. FRANK *and* MARGOT *are sleeping. He goes to the food safe and again lights a match. Then he cautiously opens the safe, taking out a half-loaf of bread. As he closes the safe, it creaks. He stands rigid.* MRS. FRANK *sits up in bed. She sees him.*

2   MRS. FRANK [*screaming*]. Otto! Otto! Komme schnell!

   The rest of the people wake, hurriedly getting up.

3   MR. FRANK. Was ist los? Was ist passiert?

   DUSSEL, *followed by* ANNE, *comes from his room.*

4   MRS. FRANK [*as she rushes over to* MR. VAN DAAN]. Er stiehlt das Essen!

5   DUSSEL [*grabbing* MR. VAN DAAN]. You! You! Give me that.

6   MRS. VAN DAAN [*coming down the stairs*]. Putti . . . Putti . . . what is it?

7   DUSSEL [*his hands on* VAN DAAN'S *neck*]. You dirty thief . . . stealing food . . . you good-for-nothing . . .

1   MR. FRANK. Mr. Dussel! For God's sake! Help me, Peter!

PETER *comes over, trying, with* MR. FRANK, *to separate the two struggling men.*

2   PETER. Let him go! Let go!

DUSSEL *drops* MR. VAN DAAN, *pushing him away. He shows them the end of a loaf of bread that he has taken from* VAN DAAN.

3   DUSSEL. You greedy, selfish . . . !

MARGOT *turns on the lights.*

4   MRS. VAN DAAN. Putti . . . what is it?

All of MRS. FRANK'S *gentleness, her self-control, is gone. She is outraged, in a frenzy of indignation.*

5   MRS. FRANK. The bread! He was stealing the bread!

6   DUSSEL. It was you, and all the time we thought it was the rats!

7   MR. FRANK. Mr. Van Daan, how could you!

8   MR. VAN DAAN. I'm hungry.

9   MRS. FRANK. We're all of us hungry! I see the children getting thinner and thinner. Your own son Peter . . . I've heard him moan in his sleep, he's so hungry. And you come in the night and steal food that should go to them . . . to the children!

10 MRS. VAN DAAN [*going to* MR. VAN DAAN *protectively*]. He. needs more food than the rest of us. He's used to more. He's a big man.

MR. VAN DAAN *breaks away, going over and sitting on the couch.*

11 MRS. FRANK [*turning on* MRS. VAN DAAN]. And you . . . you're worse than he is! You're a mother, and yet you sacrifice your child to this man . . . this . . . this . . .

12 MR. FRANK. Edith! Edith!

MARGOT *picks up the pink woollen stole, putting it over her mother's shoulders.*

1   MRS. FRANK [*paying no attention, going on to* MRS. VAN DAAN]. Don't think I haven't seen you! Always saving the choicest bits for him! I've watched you day after day and I've held my tongue. But not any longer! Not after this! Now I want him to go! I want him to get out of here!

2   MR. FRANK. Edith!
                                              } *together*
3   MR. VAN DAAN. Get out of here?

4   MRS. VAN DAAN. What do you mean?

5   MRS. FRANK. Just that! Take your things and get out!

6   MR. FRANK [*to* MRS. FRANK]. You're speaking in anger. You cannot mean what you are saying.

7   MRS. FRANK. I mean exactly that!

MRS. VAN DAAN *takes a cover from the* FRANKS' *bed, pulling it about her.*

8   MR. FRANK. For two long years we have lived here, side by side. We have respected each other's rights . . . we have managed to live in peace. Are we now going to throw it all away? I know this will never happen again, will it, Mr. Van Daan?

9   MR. VAN DAAN. No. No.

10   MRS. FRANK. He steals once! He'll steal again!

MR. VAN DAAN, *holding his stomach, starts for the bathroom.* ANNE *puts her arms around him, helping him up the step.*

11   MR. FRANK. Edith, please. Let us be calm. We'll all go to our rooms . . . and afterwards we'll sit down quietly and talk this out . . . we'll find some way . . .

12   MRS. FRANK. No! No! No more talk! I want them to leave!

13   MRS. VAN DAAN. You'd put us out, on the streets?

14   MRS. FRANK. There are other hiding places.

15   MRS. VAN DAAN. A cellar . . . a cupboard. I know. And we have no money left even to pay for that.

1   MRS. FRANK. I'll give you money. Out of my own pocket I'll give it gladly.

She gets her purse from a shelf and comes back with it.

2   MRS. VAN DAAN. Mr. Frank, you told Putti you'd never forget what he'd done for you when you came to Amsterdam. You said you could never repay him, that you . . .

3   MRS. FRANK [*counting out money*]. If my husband had any obligation to you, he's paid it, over and over.

4   MR. FRANK. Edith, I've never seen you like this before. I don't know you.

5   MRS. FRANK. I should have spoken out long ago.

6   DUSSEL. You can't be nice to some people.

7   MRS. VAN DAAN [*turning on DUSSEL*]. There would have been plenty for all of us, if *you* hadn't come in here!

8   MR. FRANK. We don't need the Nazis to destroy us. We're destroying ourselves.

He sits down, with his head in his hands. MRS. FRANK goes to MRS. VAN DAAN.

9   MRS. FRANK [*giving MRS. VAN DAAN some money*]. Give this to Miep. She'll find you a place.

10   ANNE. Mother, you're not putting *Peter* out. Peter hasn't done anything.

11   MRS. FRANK. He'll stay, of course. When I say I must protect the children, I mean Peter too.

PETER rises from the steps where he has been sitting.

12   PETER. I'd have to go if Father goes.

MR. VAN DAAN comes from the bathroom. MRS. VAN DAAN hurries to him and takes him to the couch. Then she gets water from the sink to bathe his face.

13   MRS. FRANK [*while this is going on*]. He's no father to you . . . that man! He doesn't know what it is to be a father!

1 PETER [*starting for his room*]. I wouldn't feel right. I couldn't stay.

2 MRS. FRANK. Very well, then. I'm sorry.

3 ANNE [*rushing over to* PETER]. No, Peter! No! [PETER *goes into his room, closing the door after him.* ANNE *turns back to her mother, crying*]. I don't care about the food. They can have mine! I don't want it! Only don't send them away. It'll be daylight soon. They'll be caught . . .

4 MARGOT [*putting her arms comfortingly around* ANNE]. Please, Mother!

5 MRS. FRANK. They're not going now. They'll stay here until Miep finds them a place. [*to* MRS. VAN DAAN] But one thing I insist on! He must never come down here again! He must never come to this room where the food is stored! We'll divide what we have . . . an equal share for each! [DUSSEL *hurries over to get a sack of potatoes from the food safe.* MRS. FRANK *goes on, to* MRS. VAN DAAN.] You can cook it here and take it up to him.

DUSSEL *brings the sack of potatoes back to the centre table.*

6 MARGOT. Oh, no. No. We haven't sunk so far that we're going to fight over a handful of rotten potatoes.

7 DUSSEL [*dividing the potatoes into piles*]. Mrs. Frank, Mr. Frank, Margot, Anne, Peter, Mrs. Van Daan, Mr. Van Daan, myself . . . Mrs. Frank . . .

The buzzer sounds in MIEP'S *signal.*

8 MR. FRANK. It's Miep!

He hurries over, getting his overcoat and putting it on.

9 MARGOT. At this hour?

10 MRS. FRANK. It is trouble.

11 MR. FRANK [*as he starts down to unbolt the door*]. I beg you, don't let her see a thing like this!

12 MR. DUSSEL [*counting without stopping*]. . . . Anne, Peter, Mrs. Van Daan, Mr. Van Daan, myself . . .

87

1   MARGOT [*to* DUSSEL]. Stop it! Stop it!

2   DUSSEL. ... Mr. Frank, Margot, Anne, Peter, Mrs. Van Daan, Mr. Van Daan, myself, Mrs. Frank ...

3   MRS. VAN DAAN. You're keeping the big ones for yourself! All the big ones ... Look at the size of that! ... And that! ...

> DUSSEL *continues on with his dividing.* PETER, *with his shirt and trousers on, comes from his room.*

4   MARGOT. Stop it! Stop it!

> *We hear* MIEP'S *excited voice speaking to* MR. FRANK *below.*

5   MIEP. Mr. Frank ... the most wonderful news! ... The invasion has begun!

6   MR. FRANK. Go on, tell them! Tell them!

> MIEP *comes running up the steps, ahead of* MR. FRANK. *She has a man's raincoat on over her night-clothes and a bunch of orange-coloured flowers in her hand.*

7   MIEP. Did you hear that, everybody? Did you hear what I said? The invasion has begun! The invasion!

> *They all stare at* MIEP, *unable to grasp what she is telling them.* PETER *is the first to recover his wits.*

8   PETER. Where?

9   MRS. VAN DAAN. When? When, Miep?

10 MIEP. It began early this morning ...

> *As she talks on, the realization of what she has said begins to dawn on them. Everyone goes crazy. A wild demonstration takes place.* MRS. FRANK *hugs* MR. VAN DAAN.

11 MRS. FRANK. Oh, Mr. Van Daan, did you hear that?

> DUSSEL *embraces* MRS. VAN DAAN. PETER *grabs a frying pan and parades around the room, beating on it, singing the Dutch National Anthem.* ANNE *and* MARGOT *follow him, singing, weaving in and out among the excited grown-ups.* MARGOT *breaks away to take the*

88

flowers from MIEP *and distribute them to everyone. While this pande-monium is going on* MRS. FRANK *tries to make herself heard above the excitement.*

1 MRS. FRANK *[to* MIEP*]*. How do you know?

2 MIEP. The radio ... The B.B.C. ! They said they landed on the coast of Normandy!

3 PETER. The British?

4 MIEP. British, Americans, French, Dutch, Poles, Norwegians . . . all of them! More than four thousand ships! Churchill spoke, and General Eisenhower! D-Day they call it!

5 MR. FRANK. Thank God, it's come!

6 MRS. VAN DAAN. At last!

7 MIEP *[starting out]*. I'm going to tell Mr. Kraler. This'll be better than any blood transfusion.

8 MR. FRANK *[stopping her]*. What part of Normandy did they land, did they say?

9 MIEP. Normandy ... that's all I know now ... I'll be up the minute I hear some more!

She goes hurriedly out.

10 MR. FRANK *[to* MRS. FRANK*]*. What did I tell you? What did I tell you?

MRS. FRANK *indicates that he has forgotten to bolt the door· after* MIEP. *He hurries down the steps.* MR. VAN DAAN, *sitting on the couch, suddenly breaks into a convulsive sob. Everybody looks at him, be-wildered.*

11 MRS. VAN DAAN *[hurrying to him]*. Putti! Putti! What is it? What happened?

12 MR. VAN DAAN. Please. I'm so ashamed.

MR. FRANK *comes back up the steps.*

13 DUSSEL. Oh, for God's sake!

1 MRS. VAN DAAN. Don't, Putti.

2 MARGOT. It doesn't matter now!

3 MR. FRANK [going to MR. VAN DAAN]. Didn't you hear what Miep said? The invasion has come! We're going to be liberated! This is a time to celebrate!

   He embraces MRS. FRANK *and then hurries to the cupboard and gets the cognac and a glass.*

4 MR. VAN DAAN. To steal bread from children!

5 MRS. FRANK. We've all done things that we're ashamed of.

6 ANNE. Look at me, the way I've treated Mother . . . so mean and horrid to her.

7 MRS. FRANK. No, Anneke, no.

   ANNE *runs to her mother, putting her arms around her.*

8 ANNE. Oh, Mother, I was. I was awful.

9 MR. VAN DAAN. Not like me. No one is as bad as me!

10 DUSSEL [to MR. VAN DAAN]. Stop it now! Let's be happy!

11 MR. FRANK [giving MR. VAN DAAN a glass of cognac]. Here! Here! Schnapps! Locheim!

   VAN DAAN *takes the cognac. They all watch him. He gives them a feeble smile.* ANNE *puts up her fingers in a V-for-Victory sign. As* VAN DAAN *gives an answering V-sign, they are startled to hear a loud sob from behind them. It is* MRS. FRANK, *stricken with remorse. She is sitting on the other side of the room.*

12 MRS. FRANK [through her sobs]. When I think of the terrible things I said . . .

   MR. FRANK, ANNE *and* MARGOT *hurry to her, trying to comfort her.* MR. VAN DAAN *brings her his glass of cognac.*

13 MR. VAN DAAN. No! No! You were right!

14 MRS. FRANK. That I should speak that way to you! . . . Our friends! . . . Our guests!

She starts to cry again.

1 DUSSEL. Stop it, you're spoiling the whole invasion!

As they are comforting her, the lights dim out. The curtain falls.

2 ANNE'S VOICE [*faintly at first and then with growing strength*]. We're all in much better spirits these days. There's still excellent news of the invasion. The best part about it is that I have a feeling that friends are coming. Who knows? Maybe I'll be back in school by fall. Ha, ha! The joke is on us! The warehouse man doesn't know a thing and we are paying him all that money! . . . Wednesday, the second of July, nineteen forty-four. The invasion seems temporarily to be bogged down. Mr. Kraler has to have an operation, which looks bad. The Gestapo have found the radio that was stolen. Mr. Dussel says they'll trace it back and back to the thief, and then, it's just a matter of time till they get to us. Everyone is low. Even poor Pim can't raise their spirits. I have often been downcast myself . . . but never in despair. I can shake off everything if I write. But . . . and that is the great question . . . will I ever be able to write well? I want to so much. I want to go on living even after my death. Another birthday has gone by, so now I am fifteen. Already I know what I want. I have a goal, an opinion.

As this is being said—the curtain rises on the scene, the lights dim on, and ANNE'S VOICE *fades out.*

SCENE 4

It is an afternoon a few weeks later . . . Everyone but Margot is in the main room. There is a sense of great tension.

Both MRS. FRANK *and* MR. VAN DAAN *are nervously pacing back and forth.* DUSSEL *is standing at the window, looking down fixedly at the street below.* PETER *is at the centre table, trying to do his lessons.* ANNE *sits opposite him, writing in her diary.* MRS. VAN DAAN *is seated on the couch, her eyes on* MR. FRANK *as he sits reading.*

The sound of a telephone ringing comes from the office below. They all are rigid, listening tensely. MR. DUSSEL *rushes down to* MR. FRANK.

1   DUSSEL. There it goes again, the telephone! Mr. Frank, do you hear?

2   MR. FRANK [*quietly*]. Yes. I hear.

3   DUSSEL [*pleading, insistent*]. But this is the third time, Mr. Frank! The third time in quick succession! It's a signal! I tell you it's Miep, trying to get us! For some reason she can't come to us and she's trying to warn us of something!

4   MR. FRANK. Please. Please.

5   MR. VAN DAAN [*to* DUSSEL]. You're wasting your breath.

6   DUSSEL. Something has happened, Mr. Frank. For three days now Miep hasn't been to see us! And today not a man has come to work. There hasn't been a sound in the building!

7   MRS. FRANK. Perhaps it's Sunday. We may have lost track of the days.

8   MR. VAN DAAN [*to* ANNE]. You with the diary there. What day is it?

9   DUSSEL [*going to* MRS. FRANK]. I don't lose track of the days! I know exactly what day it is! It's Friday, the fourth of August. Friday, and not a man at work. [*He rushes back to* MR. FRANK, *pleading with him, almost in tears.*] I tell you Mr. Kraler's dead. That's the only explanation. He's dead and they've closed down the building, and Miep's trying to tell us!

10 MR. FRANK. She'd never telephone us.

11 DUSSEL [*frantic*]. Mr. Frank, answer that! I beg you, answer it!

12 MR. FRANK. No.

13 MR. VAN DAAN. Just pick it up and listen. You don't have to speak. Just listen and see if it's Miep.

14 DUSSEL [*speaking at the same time*]. For God's sake . . . I ask you.

1   MR. FRANK. No. I've told you, no. I'll do nothing that might let anyone know we're in the building.

2   PETER. Mr. Frank's right.

3   MR. VAN DAAN. There's no need to tell us what side you're on.

4   MR. FRANK. If we wait patiently, quietly, I believe that help will come.

There is silence for a minute as they all listen to the telephone ringing.

5   DUSSEL. I'm going down. [*He rushes down the steps.* MR. FRANK *tries ineffectually to hold him.* DUSSEL *runs to the lower door, unbolting it. The telephone stops ringing.* DUSSEL *bolts the door and comes slowly back up the steps.*] Too late. [MR. FRANK *goes to* MARGOT *in* ANNE'S *bedroom.*]

6   MR. VAN DAAN. So we just wait here until we die.

7   MRS. VAN DAAN [*hysterically*]. I can't stand it! I'll kill myself! I'll kill myself!

8   MR. VAN DAAN. For God's sake, stop it!

In the distance, a German military band is heard playing a Viennese waltz.

9   MRS. VAN DAAN. I think you'd be glad if I did! I think you want me to die!

10 MR. VAN DAAN. Whose fault is it we're here? [MRS. VAN DAAN *starts for her room. He follows, talking at her.*] We could've been safe somewhere . . . in America or Switzerland. But no! No! You wouldn't leave when I wanted to. You couldn't leave your things. You couldn't leave your precious furniture.

11 MRS. VAN DAAN. Don't touch me!

She hurries up the stairs, followed by MR. VAN DAAN. PETER, *unable to bear it, goes to his room.* ANNE *looks after him, deeply concerned.* DUSSEL *returns to his post at the window.* MR. FRANK

93

comes back into the main room and takes a book, trying to read. MRS. FRANK *sits near the sink, starting to peel some potatoes.* ANNE *quietly goes to* PETER'S *room, closing the door after her.* PETER *is lying face down on the cot.* ANNE *leans over him, holding him in her arms, trying to bring him out of his despair.*

1   ANNE. Look, Peter, the sky. [*She looks up through the skylight.*] What a lovely, lovely day! Aren't the clouds beautiful? You know what I do when it seems as if I couldn't stand being cooped up for one more minute? I *think* myself out. I think myself on a walk in the park where I used to go with Pim. Where the jonquils and the crocus and the violets grow down the slopes. You know the most wonderful part about *thinking* yourself out? You can have it any way you like. You can have roses and violets and chrysanthemums all blooming at the same time . . . It's funny . . . I used to take it all for granted . . . and now I've gone crazy about everything to do with nature. Haven't you?

2   PETER. I've just gone crazy. I think if something doesn't happen soon . . . if we don't get out of here . . . I can't stand much more of it!

3   ANNE [*softly*]. I wish you had a religion, Peter.

4   PETER. No, thanks! Not me!

5   ANNE. Oh, I don't mean you have to be Orthodox . . . or believe in heaven and hell and purgatory and things . . . I just mean some religion . . . it doesn't matter what. Just to believe in something! When I think of all that's out there . . . the trees . . . and flowers . . . and seagulls . . . when I think of the dearness of you, Peter . . . and the goodness of the people we know . . . Mr. Kraler, Miep, Dirk, the vegetable man, all risking their lives for us every day . . . When I think of these good things, I'm not afraid any more . . . I find myself, and God, and I . . .

PETER *interrupts, getting up and walking away.*

6   PETER. That's fine! But when I begin to think, I get mad! Look at us, hiding out for two years. Not able to move!

Caught here like . . . waiting for them to come and get us . . . and all for what?

2 ANNE. We're not the only people that've had to suffer. There've always been people that've had to . . . sometimes one race . . . sometimes another . . . and yet . . .

3 PETER. That doesn't make me feel any better!

4 ANNE [*going to him*]. I know it's terrible, trying to have any faith . . . when people are doing such horrible . . . But you know what I sometimes think? I think the world may be going through a phase, the way I was with Mother. It'll pass, maybe not for hundreds of years, but some day . . . I still believe, in spite of everything, that people are really good at heart.

5 PETER. I want to see something now . . . Not a thousand years from now!

He goes over, sitting down again on the cot.

6 ANNE. But, Peter, if you'd only look at it as part of a great pattern . . . that we're just a little minute in the life . . . [*She breaks off.*] Listen to us, going at each other like a couple of stupid grown-ups! Look at the sky now. Isn't it lovely? [*She holds out her hand to him.* PETER *takes it and rises, standing with her at the window looking out, his arms around her.*] Some day, when we're outside again, I'm going to . . .

She breaks off as she hears the sound of a car, its brakes squealing as it comes to a sudden stop. The people in the other rooms also become aware of the sound. They listen tensely. Another car roars up to a screeching stop. ANNE *and* PETER *come from* PETER'S *room.* MR. *and* MRS. VAN DAAN *creep down the stairs.* DUSSEL *comes out from his room. Everyone is listening, hardly breathing. A doorbell clangs again and again in the building below.* MR. FRANK *starts quietly down the steps to the door.* DUSSEL *and* PETER *follow him. The others stand rigid, waiting, terrified. In a few seconds* DUSSEL *comes stumbling back up the steps. He shakes off* PETER'S *help and goes to his room.* MR. FRANK *bolts the door below, and comes slowly back up the steps. Their eyes are all on him as he stands there for a minute. They realize that what they feared has happened.* MRS. VAN DAAN *starts to whimper.* MR. VAN DAAN *puts her gently in a chair, and then hurries off up the stairs to their room to collect their things.* PETER *goes to comfort his mother. There is a sound of violent pounding on a door below.*

1 MR. FRANK [*quietly*]. For the past two years we have lived in fear. Now we can live in hope.

The pounding below becomes more insistent. There are muffled sounds of voices, shouting commands.

2 MEN'S VOICES. Auf machen! Da drinnen! Auf machen! Schnell! Schnell! Schnell! etc., etc.

The street door below is forced open. We hear the heavy tread of footsteps coming up. MR. FRANK *gets two school bags from the shelves, and gives one to* ANNE *and the other to* MARGOT. *He goes to get a bag for* MRS. FRANK. *The sound of feet coming up grows louder.* PETER *comes to* ANNE, *kissing her good-bye, then he goes to his room to collect his things. The buzzer of their door starts to ring.* MR. FRANK *brings* MRS. FRANK *a bag. They stand together, waiting. We hear the thud of gun butts on the door, trying to break it down.*
ANNE *stands, holding her school bag, looking over at her father and mother with a soft, reassuring smile. She is no longer a child, but a woman with courage to meet whatever lies ahead.*
The lights dim out. The curtain falls on the scene. We hear a mighty crash as the door is shattered. After a second ANNE'S *voice is heard.*

3 ANNE'S VOICE. And so it seems our stay here is over. They are waiting for us now. They've allowed us five minutes to get our things. We can each take a bag and whatever it will hold of clothing. Nothing else. So, dear Diary, that means I must leave you behind. Goodbye for a while. P.S. Please, please, Miep, or Mr. Kraler, or anyone else. If you should find this diary, will you please keep it safe for me, because some day I hope . . .

Her voice stops abruptly. There is silence. After a second the curtain rises.

SCENE 5

It is again the afternoon in November, 1945. The rooms are as we saw them in the first scene. MR. KRALER *has joined* MIEP *and* MR. FRANK. *There are coffee cups on the table. We see a great change in* MR. FRANK. *He is calm now. His bitterness is gone. He slowly turns a few pages of the diary. They are blank.*

1   MR. FRANK. No more.

He closes the diary and puts it down on the couch beside him.

2   MIEP. I'd gone to the country to find food. When I got back the block was surrounded by police . . .

3   MR. KRALER. We made it our business to learn how they knew. It was the thief . . . the thief who told them.

MIEP goes up to the gas burner, bringing back a pot of coffee.

4   MR. FRANK [*after a pause*]. It seems strange to say this, that anyone could be happy in a concentration camp. But Anne was happy in the camp in Holland where they first took us. After two years of being shut up in these rooms, she could be out . . . out in the sunshine and the fresh air that she loved.

5   MIEP [*offering the coffee to* MR. FRANK]. A little more?

6   MR. FRANK [*holding out his cup to her*]. The news of the war was good. The British and Americans were sweeping through France. We felt sure that they would get to us in time. In September we were told that we were to be shipped to Poland . . . The men to one camp. The women to another. I was sent to Auschwitz. They went to Belsen. In January we were freed, the few of us who were left. The war wasn't yet over, so it took us a long time to get home. We'd be sent here and there behind the lines where we'd be safe. Each time our train would stop . . . at a siding, or a crossing . . . we'd all get out and go from group to group . . . Where were you? Were you at Belsen? At Buchenwald? At Mauthausen? Is it

97

H

possible that you knew my wife? Did you ever see my husband? My son? My daughter? That's how I found out about my wife's death ... of Margot, the Van Daans ... Dussel. But Anne ... I still hoped ... Yesterday I went to Rotterdam. I'd heard of a woman there ... She'd been in Belsen with Anne ... I know now.

He picks up the diary again, and turns the pages back to find a certain passage. As he finds it we hear ANNE'S VOICE.

2 ANNE'S VOICE. In spite of everything, I still believe that people are really good at heart.

MR. FRANK *slowly closes the diary.*

3 MR. FRANK. She puts me to shame.

They are silent.

THE CURTAIN FALLS

Notes and Questions

'HANUKKAH!'

This is the words and music for the traditional Jewish folk song which is sung at the end of the first Act.

ALLEGRO

Oh, Han-uk-kah! Oh, Han-uk-kah! The sweet cel-e-bra-tion. A-

round the feast we gath-er In com-plete jub-il-a-tion.

Hap-pi-est of sea-sons Now is — here. Man-y are the rea-sons

for good cheer. To-geth-er We'll weath-er what ev-er to-mor-row may

bring. So hear us re-joic-ing And mer-ri-ly voic-ing The

SHOUT

Han'-uk-kah song that we sing. Hoy! So hear us re-joic-ing and

mer-ri-ly voic-ing The Han-uk-kah song that we sing.

THE DIARY

Here are the opening pages of the diary, and, for comparison with the scene on page 82, a passage from about three quarters of the way through the diary: (The actual diary can be read in Hutchinson's *Unicorn Books* and *Pan Books*.)

Sunday, 14th June, 1942

On Friday, 12th June, I woke up at six o'clock and no wonder; it was my birthday. But of course I was not allowed to get up at that hour, so I had to control my curiosity until a quarter to seven. Then I could bear it no longer, and went to the dining-room, where I received a warm welcome from Moortie (the cat).

Soon after seven I went to Mummy and Daddy and then to the sitting-room to undo my presents. The first to greet me was *you*, possibly the nicest of all. Then on the table there were a bunch of roses, a plant and some peonies, and more arrived during the day.

I got masses of things from Mummy and Daddy, and was thoroughly spoilt by various friends. Amongst other things I was given 'Camera Obscura', a party game, lots of sweets, chocolates, a puzzle, a brooch, *Tales and Legends of the Netherlands* by Joseph Cohen, *Daisy's Mountain Holiday* (a wizard book), and some money. Now I can buy *The Myths of Greece and Rome*—grand! Then Lies came to fetch me and we went to school. During break I stood everyone sweet biscuits, and then we had to go back to our lessons.

Now I must stop. Bye-bye, we're going to be great pals!

Monday, 15th June, 1942

I had my birthday party on Sunday afternoon. We showed a film *The Lighthouse Keeper* with Rin-Tin-Tin, which my school friends thoroughly enjoyed. We had a lovely time. There were lots of girls and boys. Mummy always wants to know whom I'm going to marry. Little does she guess that it's Peter Wessel; one day I managed, without blushing or flickering an eyelid, to get that idea right out of her mind. For years Lies Goosens and Sanne Houtman have been my best friends. Since then, I've got to know Jopie de Waal at the Jewish Secondary School. We are together a lot and she is now my best girl friend. Lies is more friendly with another girl, and Sanne goes to a different school, where she has made new friends.

Saturday, 20th June, 1942

I haven't written for a few days, because I wanted first of all to think about my diary. It's an odd idea for someone like me to keep a diary; not only because I have never done so before, but because it seems to me that neither I—nor for that matter anyone else—will be interested in the unbosomings of a thirteen-year old schoolgirl. Still, what does that matter? I want to write, but more than that, I want to bring out all kinds of things that lie buried deep in my heart.

There is a saying that 'paper is more patient than man'; it came back to me on one of my slightly melancholy days, while I sat chin in hand, feeling too bored and limp even to make up my mind whether to go out or stay at home. Yes, there is no doubt that paper is patient and as I don't intend to show this cardboard-covered notebook, bearing the proud name of 'diary', to anyone, unless I find a real friend, boy or girl, probably nobody cares. And now I come to the root of the matter, the reason for my starting a diary: it is that I have no such real friend.

Let me put it more clearly, since no one will believe that a girl of thirteen feels herself quite alone in the world, nor is it so. I have darling parents and a sister of sixteen. I know about thirty people whom one might call friends—I have strings of boy friends, anxious to catch a glimpse of me and who, failing that, peep at me through mirrors in class. I have relations, aunts and uncles, who are darlings too, a good home, no—I don't seem to lack anything. But it's the same with all my friends, just fun and games, nothing more. I can never bring myself to talk of anything outside the common round. We don't seem to be able to get any closer, that is the root of the trouble. Perhaps I lack confidence, but anyway, there it is, a stubborn fact and I don't seem to be able to do anything about it.

Hence, this diary. In order to enhance in my mind's eye the picture of the friend for whom I have waited so long, I don't want to set down a series of bald facts in a diary like most people do, but I want this diary itself to be my friend, and I shall call my friend Kitty. No one will grasp what I'm talking about if I begin my letters to Kitty just out of the blue, so, albeit unwillingly, I will start by sketching in brief the story of my life.

My father was 36 when he married my mother, who was then 25. My sister Margot was born in 1926 in Frankfort-on-Main. I followed on 12th June, 1929, and, as we are Jewish, we emigrated to Holland in 1933, where my father was appointed Managing Director of Travies N.V. This firm is in close relationship with the firm of Kolen & Co. in the same building, of which my father is a partner.

The rest of our family, however, felt the full impact of Hitler's anti-Jewish laws, so life was filled with anxiety. In 1938, after the pogroms, my two uncles (my mother's brothers) escaped to the U.S.A. My old grandmother came to us, she was then 73. After May, 1940, good times rapidly fled: first the war, then the capitulation, followed by the arrival of the Germans. That is when the sufferings of us Jews really began. Anti-Jewish decrees followed each other in quick succession. Jews must wear a yellow star, Jews must hand in their bicycles, Jews are banned from trams and are forbidden to drive. Jews are only allowed to do their shopping between three and five o'clock and then only in shops which bear the placard 'Jewish shop'. Jews must be indoors by eight o'clock and cannot even sit in their own gardens after that hour. Jews are forbidden to visit theatres, cinemas, and other places of entertainment. Jews may not take part in public sports. Swimming baths, tennis courts, hockey fields, and other sports grounds are all prohibited to them. Jews may not visit Christians. Jews must go to Jewish schools, and many more restrictions of a similar kind.

So we could not do this and were forbidden to do that. But

life went on in spite of it all. Jopie used to say to me: 'You're scared to do anything, because it may be forbidden.' Our freedom was strictly limited. Yet things were still bearable.

Granny died in January, 1942; no one will ever know how much she is present in my thoughts and how much I love her still.

In 1934 I went to school at the Montessori Kindergarten and continued there. It was at the end of the school year, I was in form 6B, when I had to say good-bye to Mrs. K. We both wept, it was very sad. In 1941 I went, with my sister Margot, to the Jewish Secondary School, she into the fourth form and I into the first.

So far everything is all right with the four of us and here I come to the present day.

Saturday, 20th June, 1942

Dear Kitty,

I'll start straight away. It is so peaceful at the moment, Mummy and Daddy are out and Margot has gone to play ping-pong with some friends.

I've been playing ping-pong a lot myself lately. We ping-pongers are very partial to an ice-cream, especially in summer when one gets warm at the game, so we usually finish up with a visit to the nearest ice-cream shop, 'Delphi' or 'Oasis', where Jews are allowed. We've given up scrounging for extra pocket money. 'Oasis' is usually full and amongst our large circle of friends we always manage to find some kind-hearted gentleman or boy friend, who presents us with more ice-cream than we could devour in a week.

I expect you will be rather surprised at the fact that I should talk of boy friends at my age. Alas, one simply can't seem to avoid it at our school. As soon as a boy asks if he may cycle home with me and we get into conversation, nine out of ten times I can be sure that he will fall head over heels in love immediately and simply won't allow me out of his sight. After a while it cools down of course, especially as I take little notice of ardent looks and pedal blithely on.

If it gets so far that they begin about 'asking Father' I swerve slightly on my bicycle, my satchel falls, the young man is bound to get off and hand it to me, by which time I have introduced a new topic of conversation.

These are the most innocent types; you get some who blow kisses or try to get hold of your arm, but then they are definitely knocking at the wrong door. I get off my bicycle and refuse to go farther in their company, or I pretend to be insulted and tell them in no uncertain terms to clear off.

There, the foundation of our friendship is laid, till tomorrow!

Yours, Anne

Sunday, 19th March, 1944

Dear Kitty,

Yesterday was a great day for me. I had decided to talk things out with Peter. Just as we were going to sit down to supper I whispered to him, 'Are you going to do shorthand this evening, Peter?' 'No,' was his reply. 'Then I'd just like to talk to you later!' He agreed. After the washing-up, I stood by the window in his parents' room a while for the look of things, but it wasn't long before I went to Peter. He was standing on the left side of the open window, I went and stood on the right side, and we talked. It was much easier to talk beside the open window in semi-darkness than in bright light, and I believe Peter felt the same.

We told each other so much, so very very much, that I can't repeat it all, but it was lovely; the most wonderful evening I have ever had in the 'Secret Annexe'. I will just tell you briefly the various things we talked about. First we talked about the quarrels and how I regard them quite differently now, and then about the estrangement between us and our parents.

I told Peter about Mummy and Daddy and Margot, and about myself.

At one moment he asked, 'I suppose you always give each other a good-night kiss, don't you?'

'One? Dozens! Why, don't you?'

'No, I have hardly ever kissed anyone.'

'Not even on your birthday?'

'Yes, I have then.'

We talked about how we neither of us confide in our parents, and how his parents would have loved to have his confidence, but that he didn't wish it. How I cry my heart out in bed, and he goes up into the loft and swears. How Margot and I have only really just begun to know each other well, but that, even so, we don't tell each other everything, because we are always together. Over every imaginable thing—oh, he was just as I thought!

Then we talked about 1942, how different we were then. We just don't recognize ourselves as the same people any more. How we simply couldn't bear each other in the beginning. He thought I was much too talkative and unruly, and I soon came to the conclusion that I'd no time for him. I couldn't understand why he didn't flirt with me, but now I'm glad. He also mentioned how much he isolated himself from us all. I said that there was not much difference between my noise and his silence. That I love peace and quiet too, and have nothing for myself alone, except my diary. How glad he is that my parents have children here, and that I'm glad he is here. That I understand his reserve now and his relationship with his parents, and how I would love to be able to help him.

'You always do help me,' he said. 'How?' I asked very surprised. 'By your cheerfulness.' That was certainly the loveliest thing he said. It was wonderful, he must have grown to love me as a friend, and that is enough for the time being. I am so grateful and happy, I just can't find the words. I must apologize, Kitty, that my style is not up to standard today.

I have just written down what came into my head. I have the feeling now that Peter and I share a secret. If he looks at me with those eyes that laugh and wink, then it's just as if a little light goes on inside me. I hope it will remain like this and that we may have many, many more glorious times together!

Your grateful, happy Anne

THE SET DESIGNS

The attic is a prison, and the conditions of the prison affect the characters. The scenery, therefore, is important—not just to tell us where the play takes place, but to summon up the atmosphere that could have smothered anyone less full of life than Anne, and the cramped clutter that hemmed them in.

For this edition Bill Pinner, who is resident designer at the Theatre Royal, York, has specially drawn a stage set. These designs are *not* included because they are the only, or even necessarily the best, way of solving the design problems of the text. But this is a play, and needs picturing on the stage; to produce it brings problems, and these designs show one designer's solution to them—a very vivid and atmospheric solution, as well as being one that is carefully thought out to solve the technical production problems of the need for different acting areas.

The designer's sketches are between pages 24 and 25. The first gives a general impression of the set, and shows how the stage is used to give a strong impression of height, the roofline, and the very important roofscape over the top in the background. This is an essential part of any design, for the characters in the closed-in attic are always aware of the busy German-occupied town around them. (Another approach to the design can be seen in the photograph of a London production between pages 56 and 57.)

A careful study of the scale ground plan opposite will show how it fits together, providing all the tiny acting areas, at different levels, and still allowing the audience to see the important points. 'Tormentor' is a stage designer's term for a piece of scenery which frames the stage picture, running parallel to the front of the stage. Here the tormentors are built to look like planking, and cram in the action, suggesting the roof of the building.

Drawing 4 shows how cut-away scenery can suggest, without filling in. The door into the attic room is there, but not the walls. Even the back wall is missing so that the roofscape can be fully seen. You can compare this solution to that in the set

Ground Plan for the Set

photographed between pages 56 and 57. There the peaked roofline is emphasized less, and the roofscape is around the sides of the eaves instead. Which idea makes the stage seem most closed in?

For a more simple design, ideas from both sets could be adapted. A careful comparison of the two is worthwhile. For instance, the position of the staircase from below differs. Which would be the most dramatic position?

Bill Pinner's drawings and ground plan are a realistic and practical design that can be studied in detailed comparison with the needs of the play.

QUESTIONS FOR DISCUSSION

1   What are your impressions of Anne in the first two scenes? Does she seem young for her age, or old?

2   Mr and Mrs Van Daan and Mr and Mrs Frank are to spend a long time continuously together for far longer and in far less happy conditions than most people. Does it seem by the end of Act One, Scene Two that they will get on well or not? What are the differences between the two couples?

3   Do you consider the tensions and disagreements between the members of the Frank family the normal squabbles of family life, or are they the results of their hiding?

4   Dussel was welcomed into the group by the Franks. How well does he settle in? How well do the others take to him?

5   Is Anne in any way fair in this speech? 'We're young, Margot and Peter and I! You grown-ups have had your chance! But look at us . . . If we begin thinking of all the horror in the world, we're lost! We're trying to hold on to some kind of ideals . . . when everything . . . ideals, hopes . . . everything, are being destroyed! It isn't our fault that the world is in such a mess! We weren't around when all this started! So don't try to take it out on us!' *(Page 70, Speech 3.)*

6   Looking back over the play, which things about the enforced hiding seem to you the hardest to bear?

7   In what ways has Anne changed by the end of the Play?